How-To Bamboo
Simple Instructions and Projects

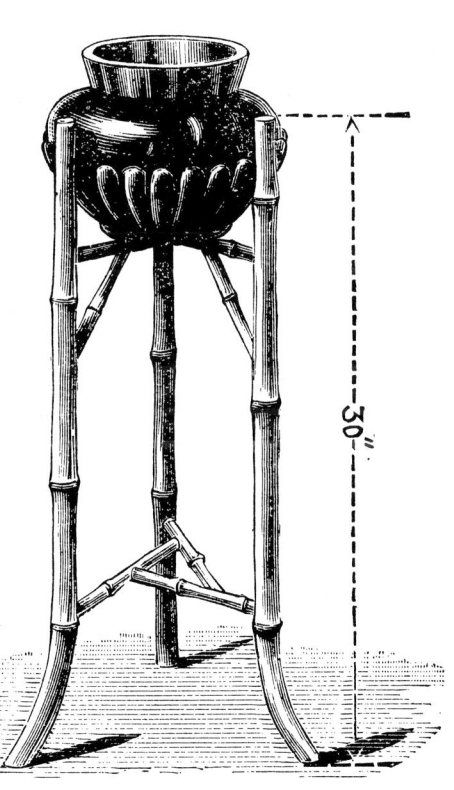

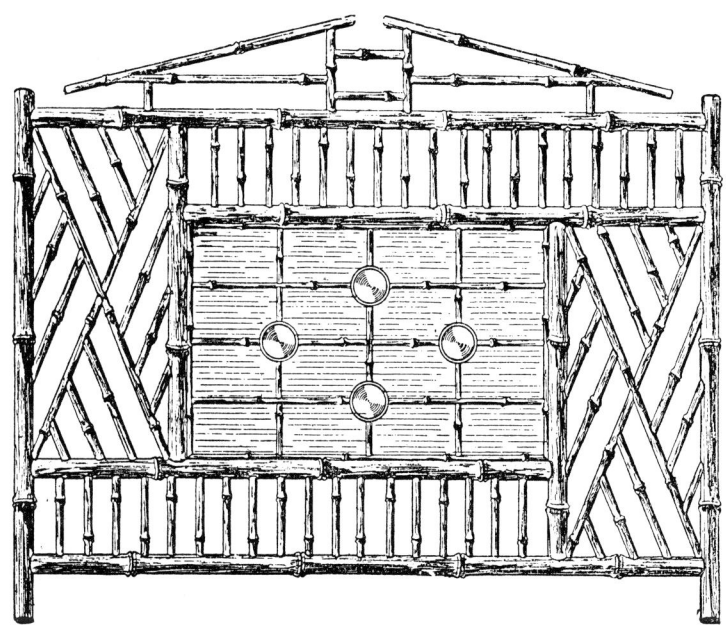

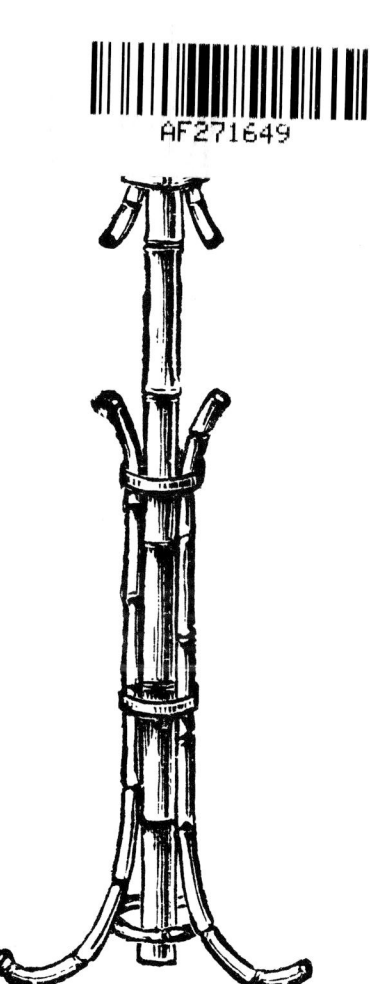

Edited by Paul N. Hasluck

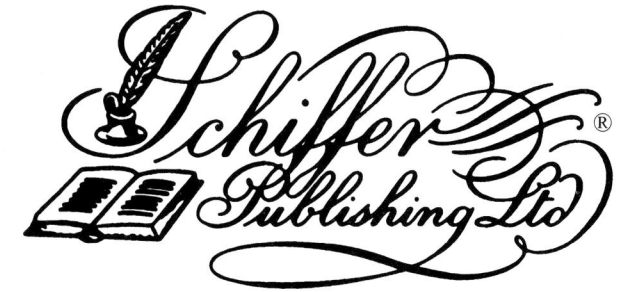

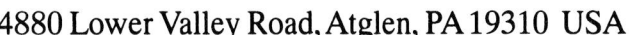

4880 Lower Valley Road, Atglen, PA 19310 USA

Published by Schiffer Publishing Ltd.
4880 Lower Valley Road
Atglen, PA 19310
Phone: (610) 593-1777; Fax: (610) 593-2002
E-mail: Info@schifferbooks.com

For the largest selection of fine reference books on this and related subjects, please visit our web site at **www.schifferbooks.com**
We are always looking for people to write books on new and related subjects. If you have an idea for a book please contact us at the above address.

This book may be purchased from the publisher.
Include $3.95 for shipping.
Please try your bookstore first.
You may write for a free catalog.

In Europe, Schiffer books are distributed by
Bushwood Books
6 Marksbury Ave.
Kew Gardens
Surrey TW9 4JF England
Phone: 44 (0) 20 8392-8585; Fax: 44 (0) 20 8392-9876
E-mail: info@bushwoodbooks.co.uk
Website: www.bushwoodbooks.co.uk
Free postage in the U.K., Europe; air mail at cost.

BAMBOO WORK.

—◆—

CHAPTER I.

BAMBOO: ITS SOURCE AND USES.

BAMBOO canes are the stems of giant grasses belonging to the genus *Bambusa* and allied genera, whose species are found in most tropical and sub-tropical regions. The allied genera include *Arundinaria*, *Arundo*, *Dendrocalamus*, *Gigantochloa*, *Melocanna*, and some others; and their species, numbering, altogether two or three hundred, if not more, may be as small and slender as pampas grass, or as large as the *Gigantochloa aspera* of Java, which in one instance was found to be 170 ft. high, and whose stem may be more than 20 in. thick.

Except only one or two species, bamboos are indigenous to some particular locality; the principal of these exceptions is *Bambusa vulgaris*, which is cultivated extensively in sub-tropical Asia, the West Indies, and South America, and which has a height of from 20 ft. to 120 ft., the stems of the larger kinds having a diameter of from 4 in. to 8 in.

All bamboo plants have stems that are very slender in proportion to their height, and these stems grow to their full length without any branches forming; when at their greatest possible height, the plants throw out straight, horizontal branches at the top, and these form a dense thicket. All bamboo plants shoot forth jointed root-stocks or rhizomes beneath the surface of the ground, and from one of these may grow from ten to one hundred stems.

The stems of bamboo plants are very strong, but hollow, with the exception of partitions at the nodes; and to these two qualities is due the great popularity and usefulness of bamboo canes, which to the Chinese, Japanese, Indo-Chinese, and West Indians are essentials to everyday life, and have been so for many centuries; to the European they have been known popularly for only a few years. Bamboo stems resemble the stems of all grasses in being jointed; they are hard, light as regards weight, elastic, and, as has been said, hollow, containing only a light, spongy pith, and the partitions at the nodes, these partitions increasing the strength of the stems greatly. Most bamboos are of approximate circular section, but one species is square; this, when three years old, has a sectional area of one square inch.

The species of *Bambusa* number about thirty; all those of imilar height have much the same appearance, the only marked difference being the stem, which varies in colour through dozens of shades, and in size from a diameter of the human finger to a diameter of twenty-two inches.

Perhaps the most beautiful and typical bamboo is *B. arundinacea*, and it is this plant that is illustrated by Fig. 1. There is little doubt but that this is one of the most useful bamboos of which the Western peoples have any knowledge.

Bamboo plants flower but rarely, but when flowering does occur, a large amount of seed results. Some of the Indian bamboos bear berries, the species noted in this respect being *Melocanna bambusoides*, on which grows an edible and fleshy fruit, from 3 in. to 5 in. long, having the shape of a pear; *M. bambusoides* grows to a height of 70 ft. or 80 ft., and attains a diameter of 12 in. Another berry-bearing bamboo is the *Nandina domestica* of China and Japan, which is used chiefly for decorative purposes, and whose berries are red.

A silicious solution contained by the stems of some bamboos, amongst them *Melocanna bambusoides*,

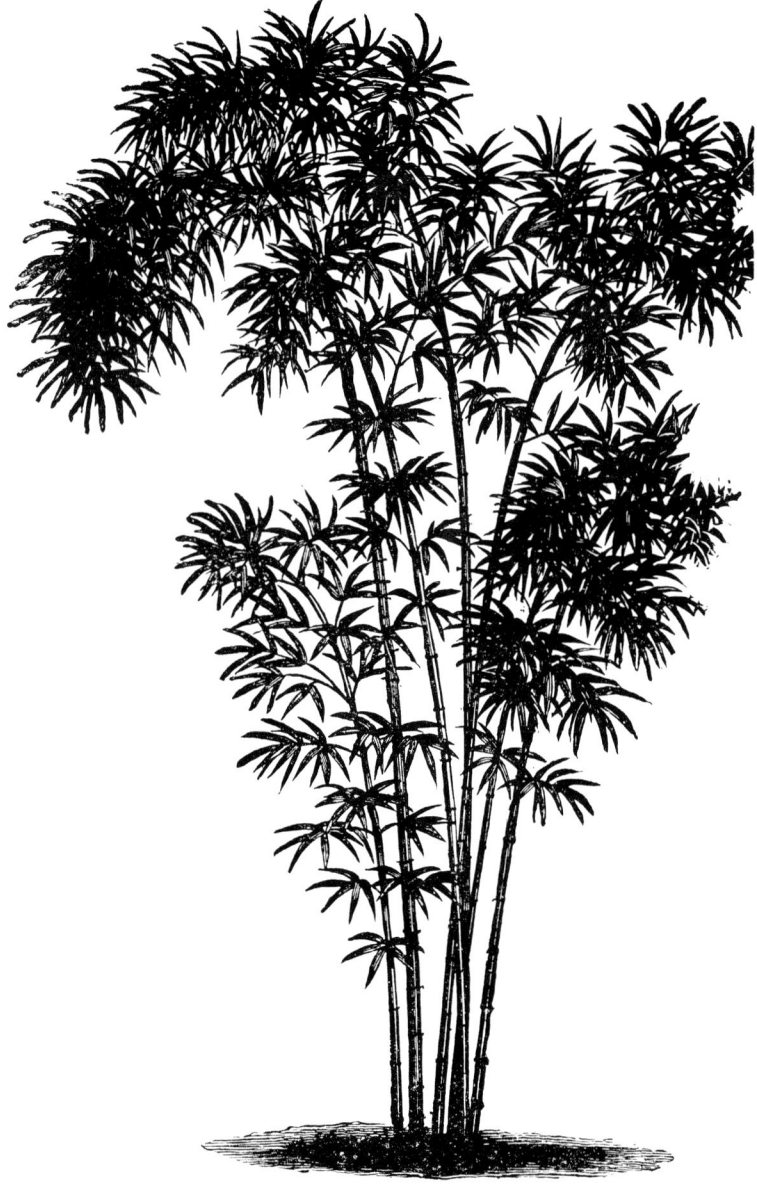

Fig. 1.—The Bamboo.

already mentioned, is known as tabasheer. This hardens to a white, opaque, or sometimes translucent, variety of opal, which breaks up into what appears to be dry starch of irregular size and shape. A suggestion has been made that the presence of tabasheer in a bamboo plant denotes disease, or is caused by some previous injury. Tabasheer will absorb its own weight of water, being then quite transparent ; calcined and powdered, it is of high esteem in India as a medicine.

It would not serve any useful purpose to tabulate here all the species of bamboo that are known ; but perhaps the names, sources, and the leading characteristics of the principal bamboo plants may be found of use. The table on the following page gives an arbitrary selection of bamboos to the number of about thirty ; the complete list would number two or three hundred.

The use of bamboo in Great Britain and the western part of Europe generally is increasing, but as yet most of its applications are in furniture making. Compared with China, Japan, India, and tropical America, its use in this country is restricted, due, of course, to its being a new material, practically. Europeans can have but little idea as to the great number of the exceedingly varied uses to which bamboo is put in the countries of its source. There is hardly any purpose for which iron, stone, or wood is used here but what is answered nearly, if not quite as well, in the Eastern countries named above by the use of bamboo.

It is interesting to give here a few brief notes descriptive of the many uses to which bamboo canes are applied, chiefly, be it said, in the East.

In China, the tender, but tasteless, bamboo shoots are used as food, being either boiled or pickled, the seeds furnishing a farina suitable for cakes. The gnarled roots are cut into fantastic carvings, or into handles for the Chinese lanterns, or are turned in a lathe to form oval sticks for the use of worshippers. The tapering canes are used for all

Species.	Sources.	Remarks.
Arundinaria japonica.	Japan and Southern England.	Dwarf species; hardy.
Arundinaria macrosperma.	North America.	10 ft. to 40 ft. high.
Arundinaria tecta.	North America,	Small or switch cane.
Arundo ampelodesmos.	South Europe and North Africa.	10 ft. high; tough flower stems and leaves.
Arundo bengalensis.	China and India.	10 ft. high; variegated white and violet leaves.
Arundo conspicua.	New Zealand and Chatham Islands.	10 ft. high; decorative plant.
Arundo donax.	Europe, North Africa, and Asia.	9 ft. or 10 ft. high; very slender reed.
Arundo karka.	Japan, China, and India.	Stem when split is material for Durma mats.
Arundo selloviana.	Lower South America.	Flowering reed; one kind of Pampas grass.
Bambusa agrestis.	South-east Asia.	Crooked and sometimes creeping stems.
Bambusa arundinacea.	India	Thorny; one of the most useful bamboos.
Bambusa bitung.	India.	Young shoots boiled for food.
Bambusa flexuosa.	China.	Dwarf species; very hardy
Bambusa guada.	South America.	Stem 16 in. in diameter and contains water.
Bambusa latifolia.	South America.	Stem contains water.
Bambusa spinosa.	Bengal.	100 ft. high; stem has thick walls.
Bambusa tabacaria.	South-east Asia.	Exceedingly hard stem.
Bambusa vulgaris.	Asia and South America.	20 ft. to 120 ft. high.
Dendrocalamus giganteus.	Malay, Archipelago.	Very tall.
Dendrocalamus hamiltoni.	Himalayas, India.	Tall; young shoots used as food.
Dendrocalamus strictus.	Malay, Archipelago.	About 100 ft. high; stem nearly solid.
Gigantochloa aspera.	Java.	Probably tallest bamboo; exceeds 150 ft. high.
Gigantochloa apus.	Indian Archipelago.	Very flexible and strong; used for ropes.
Gigantochloa maxima.	Malay, Archipelago.	Very tall and thick.
Gigantochloa nigrociliata.	India.	130 ft. to 140 ft. high.
Gigantochloa robusta.	Java.	120 ft. to 130 ft. high, 22 in. in diameter.
Gigantochloa verticillata.	India.	Tall; young shoots used as food.
Melocanna bambusoides.	India.	70 ft. or 80 ft. high; berry-bearing.

purposes that poles can be applied to in carrying, supporting, propelling, and measuring, and in all cases where strength, lightness, and length are requisite. The joists of houses and the ribs of sails, the shafts of spears and the wattles of hurdles, the tubes of aqueducts and the rafters of roofs, the handles of umbrellas and the ribs of fans, all are made of bamboo.

The leaves are sewn in layers upon cords to make rain cloaks, swept into heaps for manure, matted into thatches, or used as cloths in which to cook rice dumplings. Cut into splints and slivers of various sizes, bamboo cane is worked into baskets and trays of every form and fancy, twisted into cables, plaited into awnings for boats, houses, and streets, and woven into mats which find employment in theatre scenery, house roofs, and casings for goods of all kinds. The chips are picked into a sort of oakum and mixed with shavings to form a stuffing for mattresses. The bamboo furnishes material for the bed and the lounge, chopsticks for use in eating, pipes for smoking, flutes and other musical instruments of a like nature, curtains for windows and doors, brooms, screens, stools, coops, stands, and almost every article of furniture that can be thought of.

From bamboo is made a serviceable paper by a modern and Eastern process; but the Chinese long have had bamboo paper; and antiquaries claim that as early as 3000 B.C. the Chinese national records were written on thin plates of bamboo.

Builders' scaffolds can be made of bamboo canes, and are found light and serviceable, for the material does not decay in water or in earth, and dryness makes it harder than ever; in proportion to its weight, it is very strong. Canes 4 in. thick may be used for scaffolds 25 ft. high, and such scaffolds will bear iron beams weighing 20 cwt. Bamboo poles, suitable for scaffolds, are obtainable 65 ft. high.

It is the ease with which bamboo canes may be transformed into serviceable articles that, perhaps, is one of the chief reasons for its wide use. Bamboo can be obtained nearly 2 ft. in diameter, and a section of such a cane can be fitted very easily with a bottom and a handle to form a basket or pail, for instance. Bamboo flower pots, from 3 in. to 1 ft. in diameter, having wooden bottoms, can be constructed at something under one penny each; bamboo is very durable in damp situations, and makes almost as good a flower pot as earthenware, whilst it has not the fragile nature of this latter material. In the Castleton botanical gardens, Jamaica, are some thousands of these bamboo flower pots, which, however, have not come much, if at all, into use in Great Britain.

One curious use of bamboo is as a whetstone, another being in the making of knives. For both these purposes is required the superior kinds of bamboo having surfaces as hard as flint. *B. tabacaria* has a stem so hard that it strikes fire when cut with a hatchet.

The Annamites of Indo-China use bamboo for the making of domestic utensils, weapons of the chase and of war, furniture, water pipes, ropes, paper, and buildings. In common with the inhabitants of China and Japan, the Annamites are so skilled that they can apply bamboo canes to many of the uses for which the hardest wood or even iron or steel is considered necessary in this and in other parts of the Western hemisphere. Thus, for hydraulic and mechanical work, bamboo is made to serve, though the only available tools for preparing it are of the roughest kind. In the distilleries, where alcohol is made from rice, bamboo pipes, having joints luted with clay, conduct the spirit to and from bamboo receivers. Weaving and rope-making frames are made from bamboo, and the products of these frames probably will bear comparison with goods produced in any part of the Western hemisphere. Young and tender bamboo stalks provide food for human beings, and the leaves are eaten by horses and cattle.

Perhaps the most remarkable use of the bamboo among the Annamites is in the construction of norias; these are wheels which, during the dry season, raise water from streams and distribute it through aqueducts to the parched fields. The spot on the bank for the establishment of a noria having been selected, small dams are constructed a little higher up by planting long and substantial bamboo rods in the bed of the river so as to constitute a jetty. A passage is left free in the middle of the river so that navigation is not interrupted. In putting together a noria, two bamboo wheels, each 30 ft. in diameter, are connected together at a distance of 3 ft. apart by twenty-six paddles, alternating with twenty-six bamboo vessels arranged obliquely; the vessels are mere canes of large diameter, with one end closed. The paddles are struck by the current and cause the noria to revolve around its bamboo axle, the bearings of which are the sides of the canes in the structural support; the axle rests where certain of the canes cross each other. Each vessel in the water becomes full and is carried to the top of the wheel, but on the downward half-revolution its position, of course, is inverted, and the water flows into a woven bamboo conduit which communicates with a system of aqueducts. The speed of the wheel varies with the current, but usually the wheel revolves once in about forty seconds; and as each of the twenty-eight vessels contains about 2 qt. of water, the noria should raise about 21 gal. per minute, or 1,260 gal. per hour; in practice, not more than 18 gal. or 19 gal. would be raised per minute under such conditions. Sometimes, eight norias will work together, raising between them about 150 gal. per minute. When the current is weak the noria is made narrower, and by substituting steps for the paddles, a tread-wheel is formed, which can be worked by one coolie. Sometimes the top of the noria has a big wooden pinion which receives the motion of a horizontal wheel turned by a bullock.

The Chinese house may be bamboo from "foundations" to roof; on plan, the house is a rectangle divided into three, and the walls and two partitions are upright bamboos of large diameter, to which are lashed horizontals of the same material but smaller in diameter, still smaller canes or laths of riven cane being interlaced and plastered over with mud or clay. The door has stiles and rails of bamboo, the panels being interlaced bamboo strips. The roof is constructed by supporting bamboo purlins longitudinally on the tops of the partitions, rafters of smaller bamboos being lashed to the purlins and then overlaid with small cane, which supports a thatch of leaves obtained from the bamboo plant. The floor is of earth well rammed down.

Enough has been said to convince the reader that the possibilities of bamboo as a constructional material are practically unlimited. Though, of course, its use in this country will never be so great as in the countries of its source, yet as its properties —desirable, and indeed unique—come to be better known there can be no doubt but that it will be very generally used for many purposes for which the far more costly woods are now employed.

The supply of bamboo cannot be exhausted, for, in addition to the probable fact that its species grow over a more extended area than do those of timber trees in general, its growth is so much more rapid; whereas, timber trees are useless for constructional purposes until they are several years old, many young bamboos add from 10 ft. to 25 ft. to their height per month, and their stems are strong enough for use in but a few years.

The kinds of bamboo canes used in Great Britain and in Europe generally are black, brown, yellow, mottled, mahogany, and spotted, these colours being approximate only, and varying greatly in a bundle of canes, traded as being all of one colour. The black and mahogany canes, which are coloured artificially, are more uniform than those sold in their natural state, the yellow canes being excepted. Besides the plain stained canes, some resemble tortoise-shell with fancy mottling artificially produced, and this kind has become very popular for furniture.

The sizes of bamboo canes in ordinary use vary from $\frac{1}{2}$ in. to 3 in. in diameter, and from 18 in. to 12 ft. long; for special purposes, canes very much thicker and very much longer can be obtained. Dealers in bamboo sell the canes as a rule by the dozen or by the hundred, all of one size as nearly as possible as regards both diameter and length, but generally an assorted bundle can be obtained for a few shillings, such a bundle containing, perhaps, 150 canes ranging from 18 in. to 7ft. long, and from $\frac{1}{2}$ in. to 2 in. in diameter. Canes with roots are slightly dearer than the plain ones. Generally, bamboo dealers supply also matting, Japanese leather paper, lacquer panels and trays; from them also can be obtained the small white solid canes sometimes used for filling in open spaces in furniture instead of employing panels.

Matting, used very largely for covering the tops of bamboo tables, may be either white or fancy-coloured, and is sold by the square yard or by the roll, generally containing about 40 yards.

Japanese leather paper is sold by the roll, and may be had in many designs executed in gold, red and gold, black and gold, etc.

Japanese lacquer panels are almost a necessity in making up bamboo furniture. They are of many kinds, qualities, and sizes, the latter ranging from 15 in. square to 24 in. square, larger panels being obtainable for special purposes. These remarks on panels apply also to the shallow trays in lacquer work used for tea-tables and similar furniture.

CHAPTER II.

HOW TO WORK BAMBOO.

FURNITURE constructed of bamboo is light and dainty, and can be made by any person having a knowledge of the use of a saw, rasp, screwdriver, and chisel.

It is quite possible that some readers in their first attempt at bamboo work may meet with only slight success. Canes may split and fray up, plugs may not hold, and altogether the work may not come up to expectations, but these small difficulties should not be allowed to discourage the beginner; practice alone makes perfect, and these little experiences will impress upon the mind the three main points in bamboo work: sharp tools, hot glue, and accurate measurements. Apart from these points, of course, other little difficulties will occur, but once the worker is used to the materials he will soon be at home with the work.

In bamboo work both tools and glue should be of the best quality, and in good condition. A blunt bradawl will split the cane, a dull saw will fray it, and weak or cold glue will result in bad joints.

The outfit of tools required consists of hammer, pincers, screwdriver, tenon saw, bradawls, and, in short, of such wood-working tools as the amateur usually possesses, with the addition of a very few special ones.

Special rasps, of sharper curve than ordinary ones, are used (see the section, Fig. 2), for hollowing out the ends of bamboo canes. The requisite curve could not be obtained by using a knife. Bamboo rasps are made in all sizes from $\frac{1}{2}$ in. to $1\frac{1}{4}$ in., the most useful being $\frac{1}{2}$ in., $\frac{3}{4}$ in., and 1 in. Bamboo workers generally use a separate rasp for each size cane, as

it saves time, but a 1-in. rasp will do all the work necessary; at the same time, as rasps are not very expensive, a $\frac{3}{4}$-in. rasp can be bought, and it will be very useful.

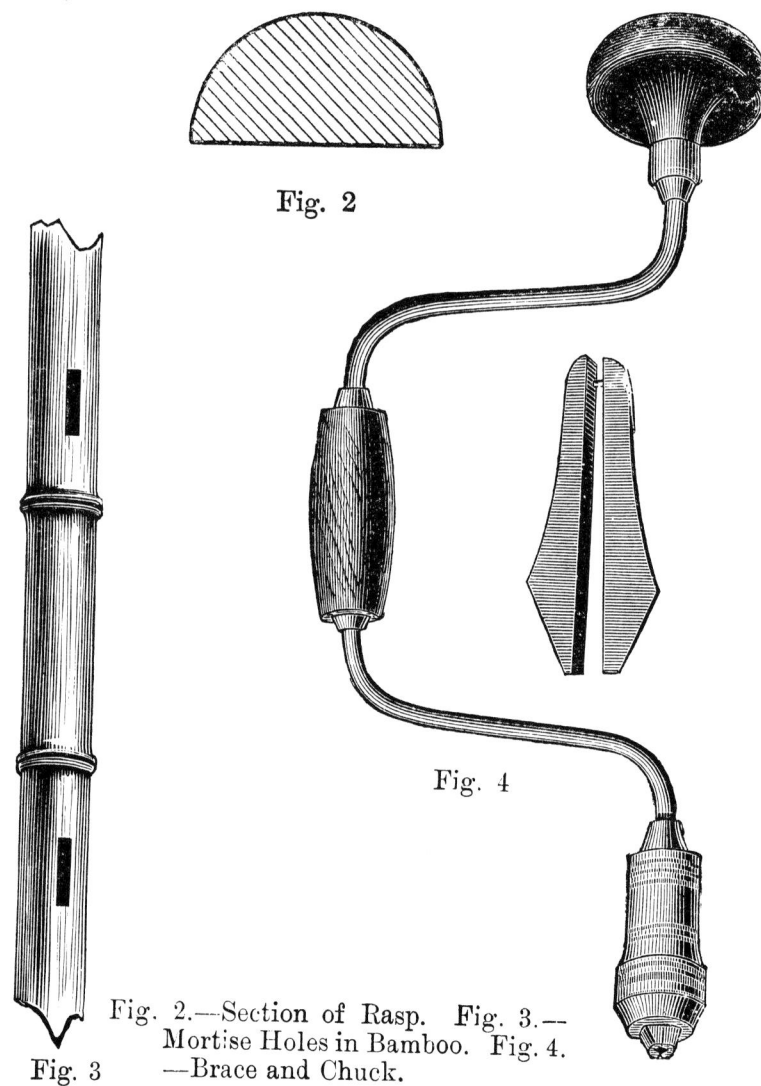

Fig. 2.

Fig. 4

Fig. 3

Fig. 2.—Section of Rasp. Fig. 3.— Mortise Holes in Bamboo. Fig. 4. —Brace and Chuck.

The ordinary tools, such as hammer, tenon saw, chisel, etc., do not need to be illustrated. A brace and a supply of drills will be necessary, because every nail that is driven into bamboo must have a hole made to receive it, or the bamboo will split. In many cases a long bradawl is a suitable tool with which to make the hole, but often the brace and bit are necessary ; the latter tools also are useful in cutting dowel or mortise holes (Fig. 3) ; the hole is

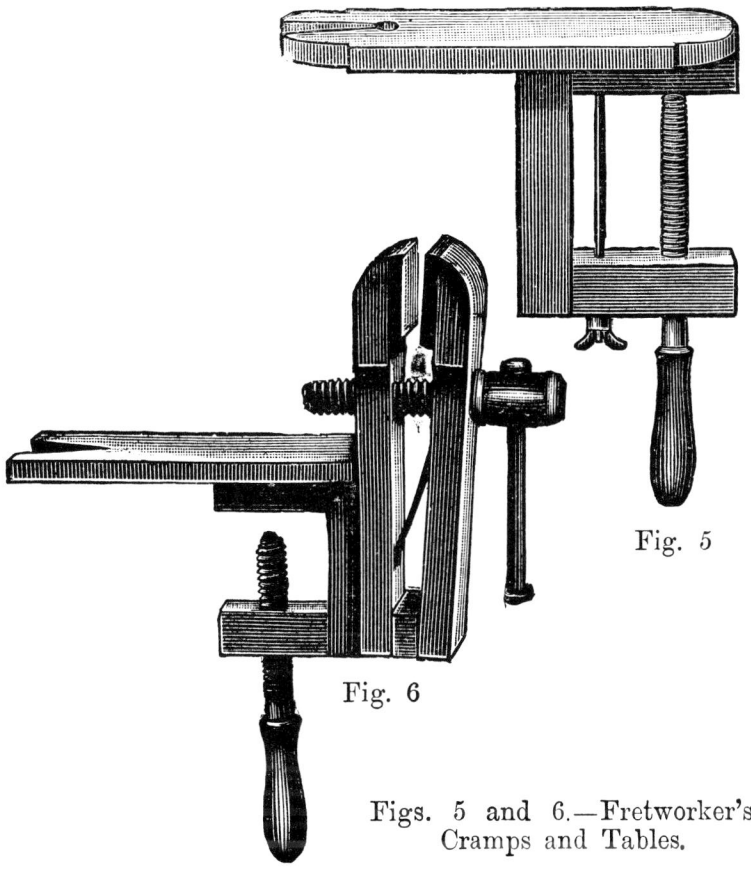

Fig. 6

Figs. 5 and 6.—Fretworker's Cramps and Tables.

started by drilling, and then is finished with the chisel, small file, or knife. The brace used may be of a simple kind ; though the American brace shown by Fig. 4 would serve the purpose well. Of course, a supply of bits to be used with the brace will be required.

A handy appliance for the bamboo worker is a fretworker's wooden cramp and table (Fig. 5),

When this appliance has a vice affixed to it as in Fig. 6 it is perhaps still handier. The cramp is fixed to any ordinary bench or table easily, and forms a most convenient work-table. A cramp and table not having a vice may be obtained in two sizes, usually ; the larger size has a table measuring $10\frac{1}{2}$ in. $\times$ $4\frac{1}{2}$ in. ; but probably it will serve the bamboo worker's purpose the better to construct such an appliance slightly larger than the one mentioned.

A board, cut as shown by Fig. 7, will be useful in rasping the ends of the canes ; it should be fixed so that the vee projects beyond the edge of the bench.

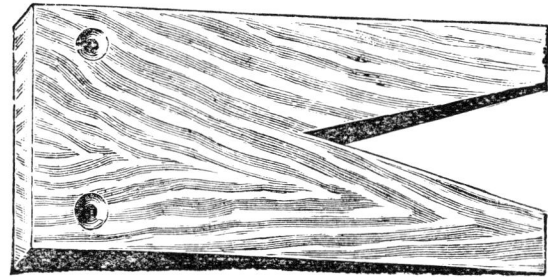

Fig. 7.—Bamboo Worker's Bench-board.

This board is not necessary if either of the fretworking appliances (Fig. 5 and 6) is obtained.

A mitre block or a mitre box will be necessary when making joints at right angles. The uneven bamboo may be rather difficult to hold true and steady on the block, but the difficulty is not so great in the mitre box, where the groove is of great assistance. An ordinary mitre block is illustrated by Fig. 8. To make it, a piece of deal, measuring $1\frac{1}{2}$ in. $\times$ 3 in. is screwed down to a piece measuring $1\frac{1}{2}$ in. $\times$ 6 in. ; both of the pieces are about 18 in. long. Then the mitre cuts at angles of 45° to the long edges are made with the saw, with which the bamboo is to be cut. The mitre box (Fig. 9) has sides 4 in. high, the strip screwed between them at the bottom being $2\frac{1}{4}$ in. wide; thus the usual sizes of bamboo canes up to 2 in. or so can be accommodated. The three pieces of wood used in making the mitre box are each $\frac{3}{4}$ in. thick, and 18 in. long. The mitre

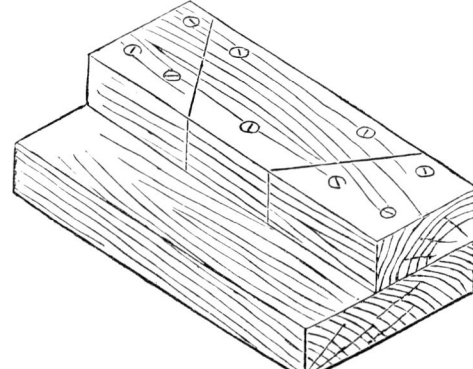

Fig. 8.—Mitre Block.

cuts are made as in the mitre block above. If canes of larger diameter than 2 in. are to be used, the width of the mitre box must be increased accordingly.

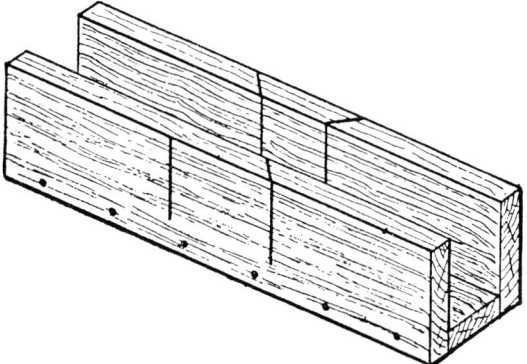

Fig. 9.—Mitre Box.

Clamps will be needed to hold together freshly glued and dowelled joints; but a good substitute for a clamp can be formed with a piece of string. As is shown in Fig. 10, the string is tied loosely round the pieces of bamboo to be held together, and

then the string is tightened by twisting, a stick being inserted for this purpose. If the stick is made just short enough to revolve in the available space, the tightened string can be prevented from untwisting by gently pushing the stick through the strings so that one of its ends rests on one of the bamboo crosspieces.

For cutting strips from bamboo canes, or for

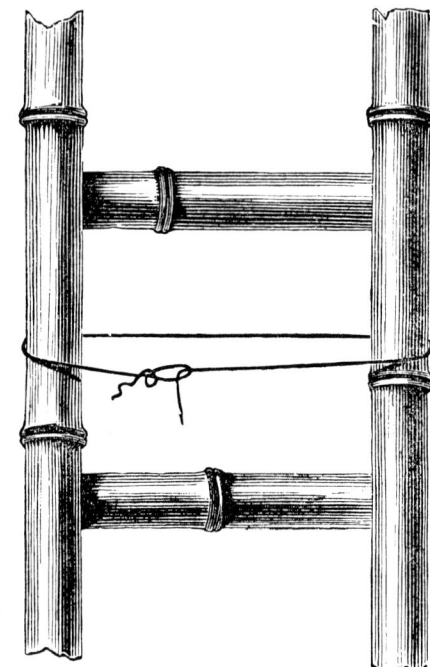

Fig. 10.—Method of Cramping Bamboo Joints.

making grooves, a cutting gauge, Fig. 11, will come in useful.

The tenon saw should have fine teeth, and should be kept well sharpened and set, the skin of bamboo being particularly hard.

The other tools or appliances required are those for use in bending bamboo chiefly. Bamboos are bent principally by heating them in a smokeless flame, the heat rendering them pliable, so that they can be bent without much difficulty, the shape given being retained when cold.

Either a Bunsen burner, if gas is available, or a

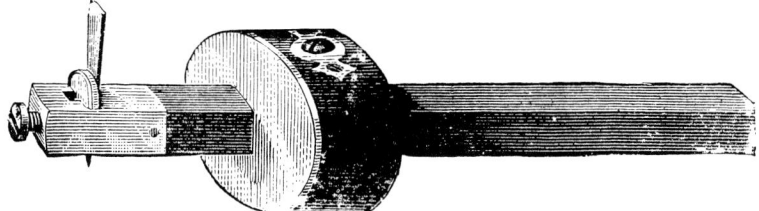

Fig. 11.—Cutting Gauge.

large spirit lamp should be obtained, though any device that gives a fairly large but smokeless flame is suitable. A plumber's benzoline blow-lamp answers admirably.

The Bunsen burner (Fig. 12) will have to be bought, probably, as will also the spirit lamp (Fig.

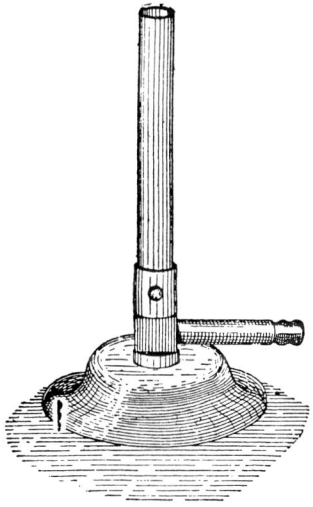

Fig. 12.—Bunsen Burner.

13) ; though a very good spirit lamp, more efficient for bamboo working than is the bought article, on account of its larger flame, can be made at home at

a cost of not more than three-halfpence. Fit a piece of bamboo, about 5 in. or 6 in. long, into the neck of a stone ginger beer bottle, and pass a wick

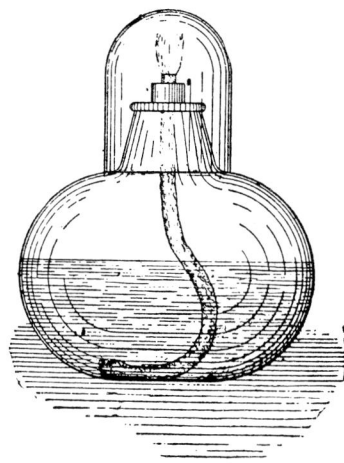

Fig. 13.—Spirit Lamp.

composed of loose cotton threads through the bamboo tube ; when the bottle has been half-filled with methylated spirit, the lamp is ready for use.

The Bunsen burner is the best possible thing for

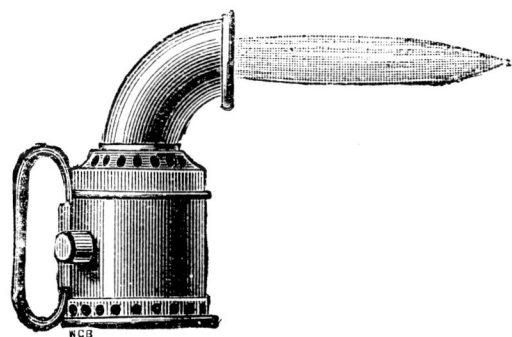

Fig. 14.—Benzoline Blow-lamp.

heating, only the heat must not be concentrated too much to one part, but the burner kept continually on the move.

A substitute for a spirit lamp or Bunsen burner is a composite candle, well wrapped round with paper from top to bottom; this, when lighted, gives a good flame, although rather smoky; but with care bamboo may be bent very well with it.

If a benzoline blow-lamp is used, it should be of simple design; that shown in Fig. 14 is as good as

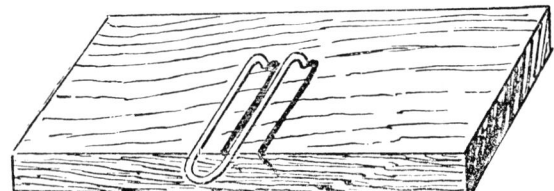

Fig. 15.—Bending-iron in Block.

any for the purpose, owing to its simplicity. Benzoline and spirit lamps, however, should be used only when there is not a gas supply, the Bunsen burner being much the best heating appliance.

A bending iron is necessary, and may be merely a piece of thick iron wire, bent as in Fig. 15, and fixed in a bench or plank; but the iron shown by

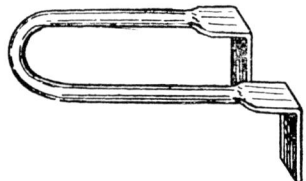

Fig. 16.—Bending Iron.

Fig. 16 is better; this is made of $\frac{3}{8}$-in. rod, the ends being flattened out, bent, and fixed in the bench as in Fig. 17. The iron loop measures 2 in. across the inside, and is from 5 in. to 7 in. long, though the size may be increased or decreased according to the size of the bamboo to be bent.

A bending iron is necessary, and it may be merely of wood may be screwed, one on the top and the other

on the bottom of the fret-cutting board (Fig. 7), as shown in Fig. 18. The strips s, which should be of tough wood, rounded a little in the middle, should be about 1 in. thick, $1\frac{1}{2}$ in. wide, and as long as the board is wide.

To bend bamboo pass the end of the cane through the loop of the bending-iron and underneath the top of the bench (Fig. 17), and with the outside end of the cane in one hand, and the Bunsen burner or other heating appliance in the other, bend the cane by a gentle downward pressure,

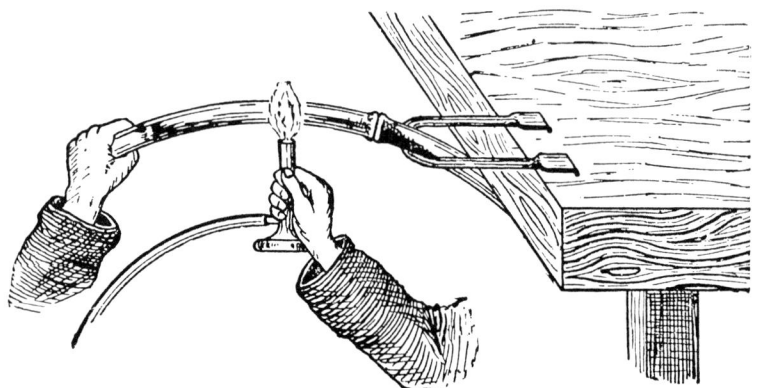

Fig. 17.—Method of Bending Bamboo.

while the part of its surface that is to form the inner curve is made hot by allowing the flame to play upon it as it is passed slowly up and down (see Fig. 17). Do not concentrate the heat, but move the flame about so that the cane is not burnt. When the cane is sufficiently pliable, a gentle pressure should be able to produce the required curve; then a wet cloth should be rubbed up and down the cane till it is cold, keeping the cane in the bending-iron and continuing the downward pressure. Canes that have been exposed very long to the weather, or that are old, can seldom be bent satisfactorily. Fresh, new canes as just imported bend the best.

When a sharp bend is required it will be better

to cool down as above described when it is bent to half the requisite curve, and resume the heating and bending after sufficient time has been allowed for the cane to cool. A cane that is bent too quickly is liable to split

When heating preparatory to bending take care not to burn the canes; revolving them will prevent this. It is best to make the bend on a part of the bamboo between the knots. But if there must be a knot where the bend is required, rasp the knot flat on the side that will form the inside of the bend, and (excepting in very thin canes) notch on the same side with a saw about a quarter through. In

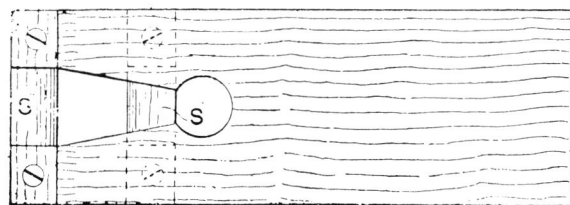

Fig. 18.—Bending-board for Bamboo.

any case, it will assist the bending operations if a few very slight saw cuts are made on the inner part of the cane required to be bent. This prevents the surface of the cane breaking away. It is not quite possible to prevent a certain amount of flattening at the bend; but this can be remedied to a great extent by using a mallet judiciously when the bend is thoroughly set, and the inner parts, where joined on to other parts, may be slightly rasped to restore the requisite roundness. If a bend is made too acute, it can be opened out by heating in the flame and pulling apart in the hands, or in the bending hook. It is not possible to bend a bamboo cane to a very acute angle without cutting out a **V**-shaped piece to allow for the reduced length of the inner as compared with the outer side of the cane. A slight

bend is all that can be made if the cane is to be uninjured or uncut. The bending must be done very gradually. It is better to go by easy stages if the cane is very large, hard, or tough. Of course, very large and thick canes can scarcely be bent at all. Canes stouter than $1\frac{1}{4}$ in. or $1\frac{3}{8}$ in. cannot be bent satisfactorily; here, joints must be made to serve the purpose.

When several pieces of bamboo are to be bent to a uniform curve, the only method is to bend the

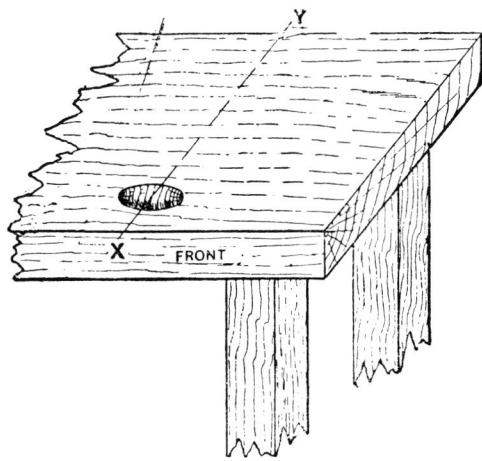

Fig. 19.—Bamboo Worker's Bench.

first piece to the required shape and then to use it as a pattern, the other bends being tested by it. If a complex bend is required, a drawing is often made on a piece of wood or paper, and the bend applied to the drawing as the work proceeds.

Cane $\frac{3}{8}$ in. in diameter may be bent into small scrolls in the following manner. Soak the cane in water for twelve or more hours, and then hold over a Bunsen flame. When supple, wrap the cane round a peg of the size wished, and tie it there till cold.

Many professional bamboo workers, instead of using a bending iron, have a 2-in. hole, as shown in Fig. 19 bored slantingly through a very strong bench ; the inclination of the hole is shown by Fig. 20, which is a section on line x y (Fig. 19). The cane to be bent is inserted in the hole and treated as usual. This is claimed to be the best method of bending, as when using a bending-iron there is a liability of this getting too hot, and so marking the cane. The canes to be bent should be heavy, though not more than $1\frac{3}{8}$ in. in diameter, as the more substantial are less liable to bulge or split than the lighter ones.

It is difficult to bend bamboo by the usual method without the flame marking it ; but a method

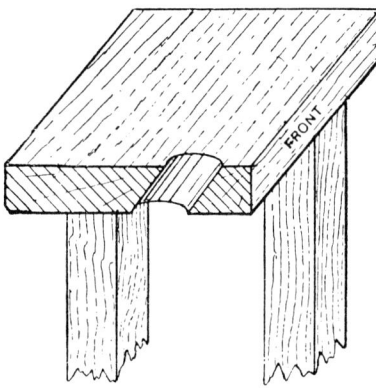

Fig. 20.—Section of Bench.

which answers when the canes must not be marked is to soak them in boiling water, and whilst hot to bend them as required. When cold the cane will permanently have assumed the shape given it.

Bamboo canes may be rendered sufficiently supple for being bent by steaming ; the time taken to soften the bamboo can be shortened by employing superheated steam. The bamboo is placed in the steaming apparatus, the lid screwed close, and the steam turned on. When the bamboo is softened, the steam is turned off ; directly the bamboo is removed from the steam, it must be bent, and held so until cold.

A steam chest for bamboo is illustrated by Fig. 21.

The chest is made as follows :—Procure four pieces of sound deal, 1 ft. wide by $1\frac{1}{2}$ in. thick, and about 3 ft. 6 in. long. Join the edges of these together, as shown at Fig. 22, to form a box, firmly screwing the joints and bedding them with thick white lead. Close one end with a block firmly secured with screws, and make a lid for the other end, as shown at Fig. 21. The lid is a block a little larger than the sectional area of the chest, with pieces fixed to the sides to fit over the end of the chest. On each side of the chest the lid is secured by a strap-bolt, the screwed end of which passes through the lid, and is fastened by a cross-plate and

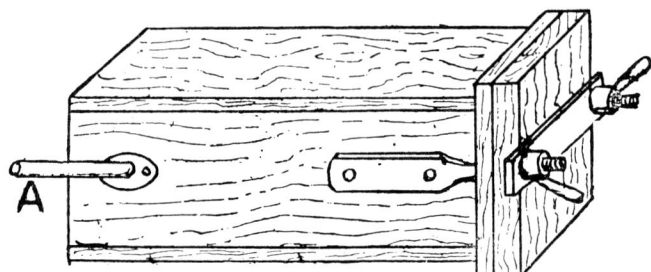

Fig. 21.—Steam-chest for Bamboo.

two wing-nuts. The chest is connected to a steam boiler by a small steam pipe, as shown at A (Fig. 21). Place the wood in the chest, turn on the steam, and proceed as before described. Do not screw on the lid too tightly, but allow it to "blow" a little. It must be remembered that though steam bending is commonly employed for ordinary woods, professional bamboo workers but rarely make use of it. The Bunsen burner and the bending iron give better results at less expense of money and of time. The steam method might have advantages for repetition work, but it is doubtful whether the amateur will find it of any use at all.

The beginner probably will split many canes in his first attempts at bending. This is due, perhaps, to too much heat, and consequent burning, or to insufficient heat, in which case the cane does not become pliable enough. Or perhaps the cane has been bent too quickly; a usual fault is that the heat is concentrated too much. A safe plan is to apply heat over a considerable surface and keep the burner constantly on the move, then, with one hand holding the end of the cane, by putting the pressure on gradually the cane will give slightly. Occasionally wipe the part heated with a wet rag, still keeping the cane bent; then apply more heat and again the wet rag, and so on until the required bend is obtained.

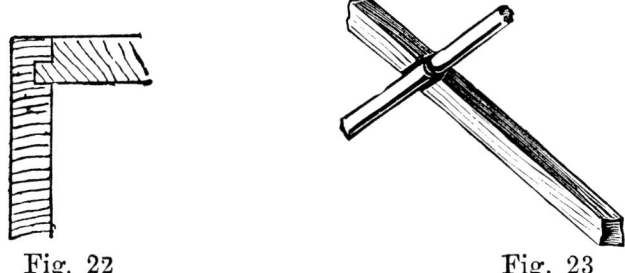

Fig. 22   Fig. 23

Fig. 22.—Joint of Steam-chest. Fig. 23.—Method of Straightening Bamboo.

As has been said, canes may be straightened in the same way that they are bent; a very convenient tool for straightening bamboo is a piece of deal about 2 in. square and about 16 in. long, with a square groove, $1\frac{1}{2}$ in. wide and 1 in. deep, cut obliquely across one of its sides (Fig. 23). The cane to be straightened must first be made hot in the flame of a Bunsen burner, then laid in the groove, by which it will be gripped, while the wooden tool is used as a lever to straighten it.

The joints used in bamboo work are only a few in number. For joining the ends of two canes together at right angles, in all cases a mitred joint is the most satisfactory and easiest in working, and should be adopted wherever practicable, leaving the bends

for flowing lines and curves, as shown in the many examples given in the following pages. In forming a mitred joint, the ends of the two canes are plugged with pieces of wood which are glued in. When the glue is quite hard, the mitres are cut on a mitre block or in a mitre box with a tenon saw, and

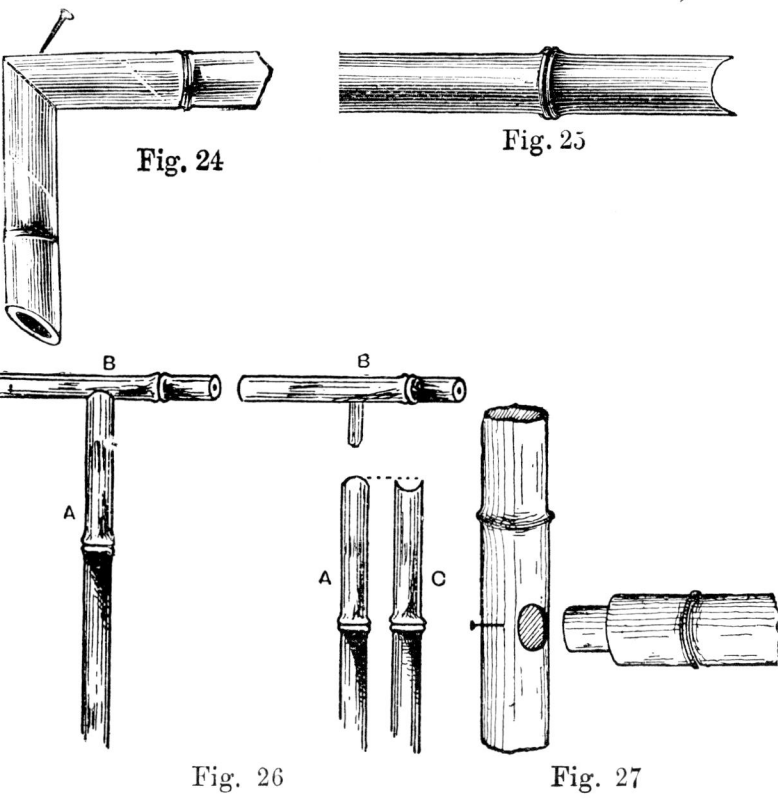

Fig. 26   Fig. 27

Fig. 24.—Mitred Joint in Bamboo. Fig. 25.—Hollowed End of Cane. Figs. 26 and 27.—Tee Joints in Bamboo.

the two sawn surfaces then are placed together, glued, and further secured by fine nails or brads, in the way shown by Fig. 24.

When a piece of bamboo is to be joined to another piece at right angles to form a T, the end of one piece is rasped out to fit the curvature of the other (see Fig. 25). Either before or after rasping, the end is plugged. In this case the two pieces are held together merely by a nail passing through one cane into the plugged end of the other. Fig. 26 shows a better method of making such a joint. The hole, at the end of A is smoothed 2 in. or 3 in. deep to receive the dowel fixed in B, after which the end is rasped out as shown at C, so that it fits evenly on B. Glue should be used to make the joint secure. Another method, but one, however, which practically is the same as the last, is to drill a hole in the side of one piece, and to insert in this the plugged end of the other; secure with a wire nail (see Fig. 27).

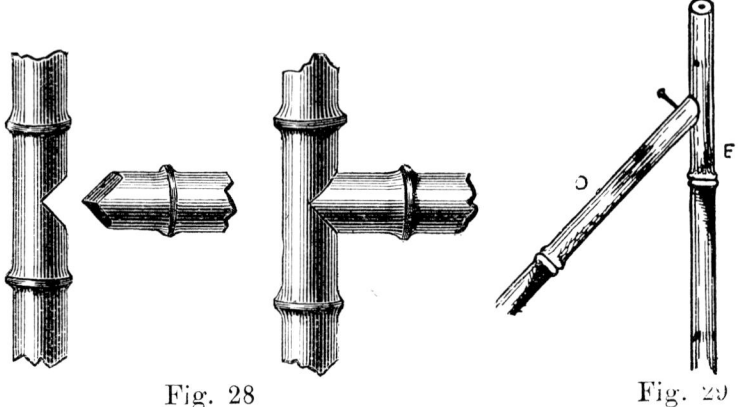

Fig. 28

Fig. 29

Fig. 28.—Tee Joint in Bamboo. Fig. 29.—Angle Joint in Bamboo.

The best wood for dowels is straight-grained deal; this is sawn into long, square strips, and cut up into the special short lengths required, being shaped to fit the hollow canes by means of a knife, plane, or chisel.

Another method of forming a T-joint is shown in Fig. 28. The end of one piece is plugged and shaped as shown. A vee-piece is cut in the other, and the joint made with glue and a fine nail.

Pieces joining at an angle other than a right angle are illustrated by Fig. 29. Cut the end of the cane D to the proper angle, plug it with a piece of wood,

and then round it off with the rasp so that it fits evenly against the cane E. At the connecting point sandpaper the varnish off the vertical bamboo rod, the glue holding better when the cane is thus roughened. The joint can be further strengthened by means of a nail or screw, as shown.

Fig. 30 illustrates the joint of diagonal pieces. This is made in much the same way as described for the joint illustrated by Fig. 26, the ends of the two shorter rods being bored to receive the ends of

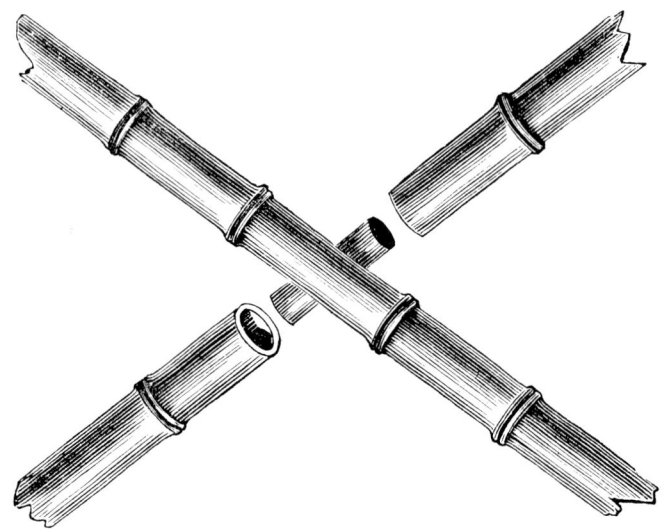

Fig. 30.—Diagonal Joint in Bamboo.

the dowel, which passes quite through the longer cane, a hole having been bored to receive it.

Lengths of bamboo are jointed one to the other in a straight line, either by glued plugs or by brass ferrules. In joining two lengths at an angle it is better to cut off one piece at the knot, as any difference in the thickness can then easily be rasped off. The bay-pole joint shown by Fig. 31 saves a lot of trouble in such a case. It is really a cup and ball joint, and is made of wood, tortoised to imitate bamboo; at each end is an iron screw (wood thread) and all that is to be done when forming the joint is to cut the bamboo the requisite length, allowing for the joint, plug the ends with wood, and screw the joint into them. They not only make the bay-pole strong where the weakest point generally is, but no template is required, as these joints adjust themselves to any angle.

In running a rebate in a bamboo cane an ordinary rebate plane may be used. The principal difficulty,

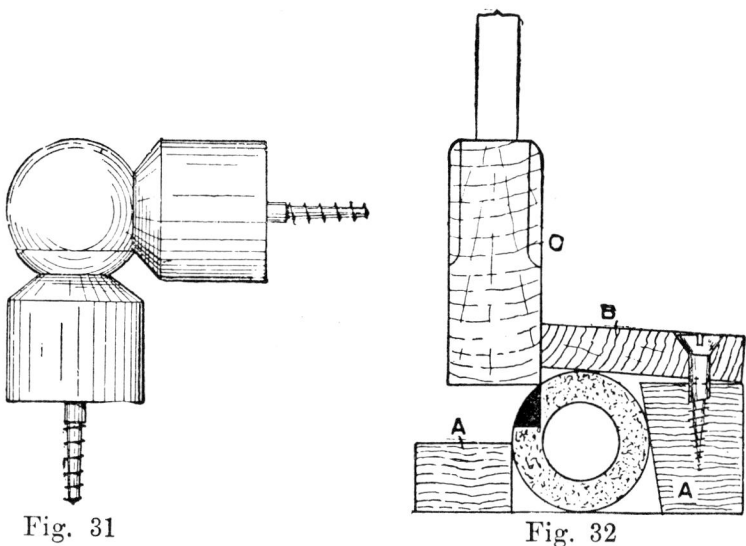

Fig. 31   Fig. 32

Fig. 31.—Bay-pole Joint.   Fig. 32.—Method of Rebating Bamboo.

however, will be in the holding of the material while using the plane ; but this can be overcome by proceeding as follows :—Secure a few little blocks to the bench on each side of the cane as at A A, Fig. 32, screw a lath with one of its edges straightened on to the blocks, to press tightly on the top of the cane, as at B. The edge of this will form a guide for the rebate plane C, and will enable the worker easily to clean out the portion shown in black on Fig. 32. If the rebate groove is to be "stopped" within a few inches of each end, it may be cleaned

out with a chisel, and finished with a router, or "old woman's tooth plane," using the lath B in this case as a guide for both width and depth.

If it is desired to remove knots from the inside of a length of bamboo to transform it into a tube an iron rod may be made red hot and passed through the bamboo. The thin knots in the inside by this means should be burnt through.

Bad joints in bamboo work can be filled in with a mixture of sawdust and hot glue made to the consistency of thin paste, all surplus paste being cleaned off before it dries. Cracks in bamboo canes can be filled with shoemakers' heelball. A lighted taper is applied to the heelball, and sufficient allowed to drop into the flaw. After it has set, rub with a clean cloth until the surface is perfectly level. Another mixture for filling in bad joints is one made by melting equal parts of resin and beeswax in an old ladle or spoon ; yellow ochre or umber is added to match the colour of the bamboo. Press the composition well in with a piece of wood, and clean off when cold with a sharp knife or chisel. Touch up afterwards with transparent spirit varnish. A filling for screw holes in bamboo is plaster of Paris, mixed with water and applied immediately it is made. When dry it can be glass-papered smooth and coloured with dragon's blood, gamboge, etc. ; or ochres and umbers can be mixed with the wet plaster to give the desired tints.

Yellow bamboo cane is mottled or marked by burning at frequent intervals with a Bunsen burner, or by partly covering the cane with a thin paste of whiting and water, and then passing the cane through a flame, afterwards removing the whiting. The paste protects the covered parts from burning. Tortoiseshell bamboo canes are so cheap, however, that it does not pay to mottle the yellow ones.

Light canes are darkened by scorching them in the flame of a Bunsen burner or spirit lamp. Another way is to coat them with ordinary enamel paint. In the trade, to brighten the colour a hard varnish is used diluted with an equal bulk of methylated spirit. Bamboo will not take stain or dye as does ordinary wood; so any colour that cannot be obtained by scorching the cane must be applied in the form of coloured varnish. Professionals generally colour bamboo furniture after it is made up by applying suitable pigments, as vandyke brown, brown umber, or black mixed with French polish or spirit varnish thinned out with methylated spirit, finishing with clear varnish. Light coloured canes that have been stored in a damp place to render them soft may be stained brown with a mixture of vandyke brown and American potash in hot water.

A transparent varnish for bamboo is made by dissolving 3 oz. of white shellac in 10 fluid oz. of methylated spirit; this is applied to the bamboo with a camel-hair brush. Any good white shellac varnish is suitable, or the following will give good results:—(1) Dissolve 4 oz. of fine picked gum sandarach in 1 pt. of methylated spirit, and, after straining, add 2 oz. of finest pale turpentine varnish. (2) Dissolve 2 oz. of powdered bleached shellac in two-thirds of a pint of methylated spirit, and then filter to arrest any impurities that were present in the shellac; then add very gradually one-third of a pint of methylated spirit. A cheap varnish suitable for bamboo work may be made with common shellac, 8 oz.; gum thus, 2 oz.; resin, 2 oz., and methylated spirit, 1 qt. This can be sponged on, instead of brushed on, if desired.

Bamboo can be darkened by coating it with a dark varnish made according to recipe No. 2 above, substituting, however, orange, or a still darker shellac for the bleached shellac there mentioned.

To colour ordinary wooden sticks to match bamboo give them a rubber of polish or coat of spirit varnish to impart a yellow tint and stop suction.

Mix some vandyke brown in spirit varnish, and mix the latter in spirit till it gives the tone required; then stipple on with a camel-hair brush, the gradations of tone and knotty appearance being gained by dabbing the colour on several times where required. When dry smooth with fine, worn glasspaper or coarse rag, and coat with spirit varnish; apply carefully so as to prevent the colour running.

As so many of the joints in bamboo work depend upon the adhesive power of glue, every care should be taken that this is of good quality, and is made properly. The natural enamel on bamboo canes is not conducive to strength when glue is used on joints, and so this hard enamel should be rasped off before applying the glue. Much depends, also, upon the manner in which the glue is made. It does not suffice to place the glue in water, and at once bring to the boil. The proper way of making glue is first to break the cakes of glue into small pieces; place the broken glue in the glue-pot or in a gallipot, and cover with water. Put aside for about six hours; if after an hour or so all the water is absorbed, add some more. At the end of the six hours, pour off any unabsorbed water, place the vessel in a water-bath, and gently boil for a short time, or until the glue is all dissolved, and forms a quickly-running liquid. Use it as hot as possible. Do not boil the same glue more than twice, as then its strength goes. After the first boiling, allow to get cold, and form a jelly; then, as it may be required, pieces of the jelly may be cut off and heated. Thus a stock of reliable glue is always at hand. The cake glue should be nearly transparent, with but little taste or smell, free from spots or cloudiness, and of a deep brown colour. The adhesive power of bone glue is in proportion to its consistency and elasticity after it has been soaked in water for some hours and has absorbed many times its own weight of the water.

CHAPTER III.

BAMBOO TABLES.

A VERY favourite employment for bamboo, and one for which the canes are admirably fitted, is the construction of fancy tables. With the aid of some few supplementary materials, can be made a large variety of tables, including afternoon tea tables, plant tables, work-tables, etc.

Bamboo furniture is in itself very artistic, and is much seen in recently furnished houses, more especially in drawing-rooms, where a touch of Eastern art is given by the many coloured silks and Japanese fans; if strongly and carefully made, bamboo furniture will be found very durable indeed, as well as handsome, and will well repay the trouble of making.

In the instructions to be given in this and following chapters, it is assumed that the reader has mastered the elements of cane-bending and joint-making, upon which information is given in Chapter II. Limitations of space will not allow the repetition of this instruction; therefore, as the examples of bamboo work are briefly described and illustrated in succession, the reader must refer for details of the practical work and processes to the explanations given in the second chapter.

A simply-made bamboo table is illustrated by Fig. 33. It consists of three Japanese lacquered trays, A, B, and C, each 18 in. square, with four uprights of bamboo about 1 in. thick and 28 in. long. Bend out the legs at the bottom as described in Chapter II., and straighten the canes, if required. Mark the canes at distances of 10 in. and 20 in. from the top, and saw each one quite squarely into three pieces, being careful to keep the pieces of

each cane by themselves, because the least slant will spoil the work. With a brace and bit about the size of the dowel it will be necessary to use, bore holes

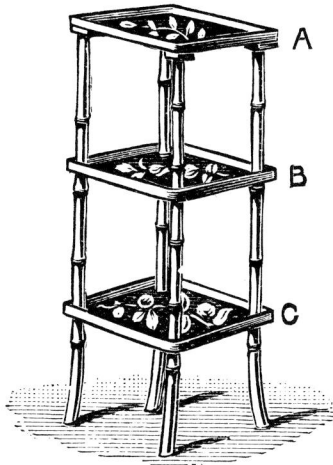

Fig. 33.—Three-tray Bamboo Table.

in the four corners of two of the trays. Take the four portions of bent cane that are to form the legs, and into their top ends fit dowels, which must

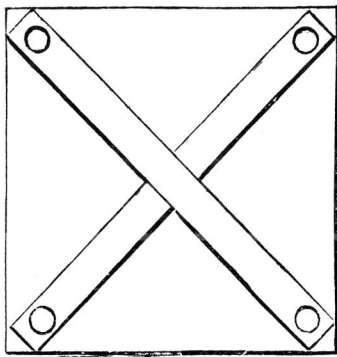

Fig. 34.—Support for Table Top.

project about 3 in.; put each dowel through the holes bored in the tray, glue the parts, and join on the middle lengths of bamboo. Put dowel pins in the tops of these, and fit on the next tray, and then the other four lengths ; the tops of these last lengths should be plugged, but the plugs should not project. Cut two pieces of deal about ½ in. thick and 2 in. wide, as shown in Fig. 34. With brace and bit bore holes half through to take the tops of the bamboo rods, which should fit in tightly ; glue in position. Glue on the top tray, holding it in its place with a pair of joiners' hand-screws until set.

Another example is shown by Fig. 35 ; the frame of this should be made of about 1¼ in. bamboo rods,

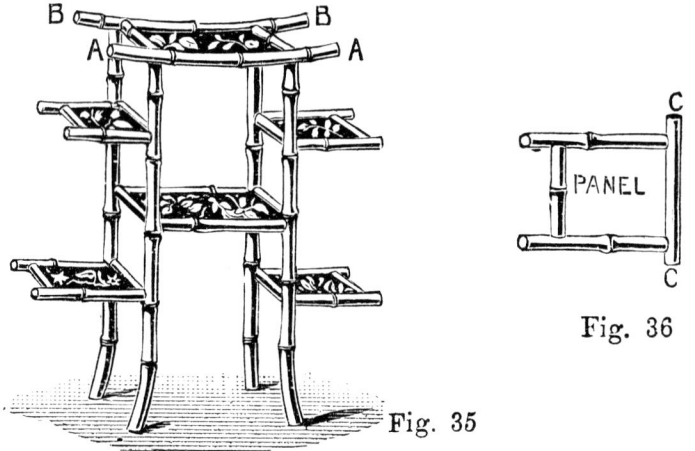

Fig. 35.—Bamboo Table with Shelf Brackets.
Fig. 36.—Shelf Bracket for Table.

and the projecting shelf brackets of about 1 in. rods. The following are suitable measurements : height, 28 in. ; length, 21 in. ; depth, 12 in. ; shelf brackets, 10½ in. square. The table is made with the two sides forming flat sections, A A and B B. The four shelf brackets should now be made, and Fig. 36 shows their construction. The cross-bars for joining the two flat sections together should be cut and plugged, and as these should be of ¾ in. bamboo, it would be better to bore holes and fit them to the sections direct, similarly with the shelf brackets. A screw with head countersunk will hold each corner secure. It is advissble to fix the panels direct into the

frame by taking out a section of the cane just sufficient for the panels to fit in ; or they can be beaded in with rattan cane. The projecting ends of the table top should be 3 in. long, and be plugged and finished with hardwood terminals. A pretty finish

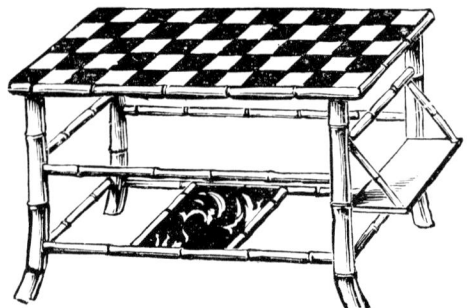

Fig. 37.—Bamboo Occasional Table with Flap.

to this table can be given by gilding the knots or by applying gold paint ; if preferred, instead of panels, plain wood can be used, and this may have a coat of enamel paint to harmonise with the colour of the rest of the table.

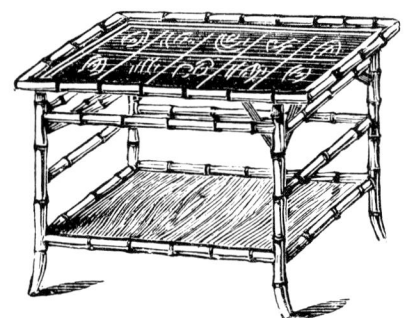

Fig. 38.—Bamboo Table with Shelf.

Tables or other bamboo structures that are top-heavy have holes drilled in the lower ends of the legs and moulten lead poured in. Plaster of Paris may replace lead for this purpose.

For the occasional table shown by Fig. 37 use stout bamboos for the legs, and smaller canes for the cross-pieces. These latter can be inserted into holes bored into the legs, and then glued and pinned. The legs may be plugged at the bottom if desired, or canes with roots may be used. The top can be of deal or pine, covered with Japanese matting, the legs being let into holes. If the top has battens at the ends these will add strength, and form a better holding substance in which the legs can fit. The flap is supported as described on p. 52. Papier-mâché trays make excellent shelves for this purpose.

The table shown by Fig. 38 may conveniently

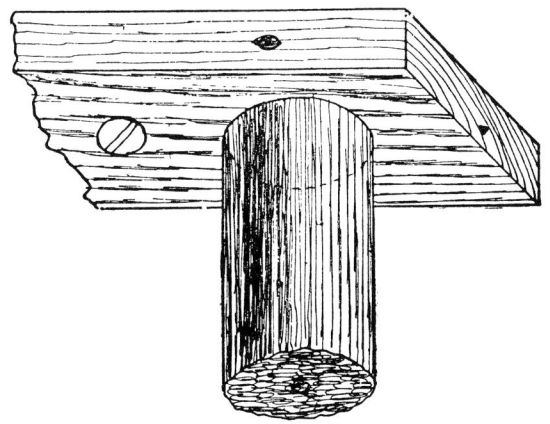

Fig. 39.—Top Batten and Leg of Bamboo Table.

have a length of 3 ft., a width of 2 ft., and a height of 2 ft. 7 in. It has so much in common with other tables described in this chapter that it is not necessary to describe its construction in detail; its top is a lacquer panel, or it may be of wood covered with fancy tiles; the shelf is of thin wood, stained and varnished, or it may be another panel.

Tables having tops framed in bamboo may have the legs attached to them in the following way:— The table top rests on strips of deal or other suitable wood, in which are bored holes to receive the top ends of the legs, which are glued and fastened with a sprig as indicated in Fig. 39. The strips should

be halved and glued together where it is necessary to join them, and they then are secured to the under-side of the top with a few screws. The halving of one of the strips is shown at Fig. 40.

The corners of a bamboo hexagon-shaped table top are cut on a special mitre block, and the

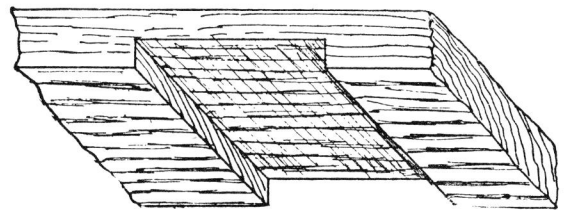

Fig. 40.—Halved Batten for Bamboo Table Top.

simplest way of cutting the mitres is to construct a mitre block as shown by Fig. 41, having its saw kerfs at an angle of 60°, as indicated. It is only in the angle of the saw kerfs that this block differs from the one shown by Fig. 8, p. 23.

The bamboo occasional table illustrated in elevation by Fig. 42 is made chiefly of $1\frac{1}{2}$-in. bamboo.

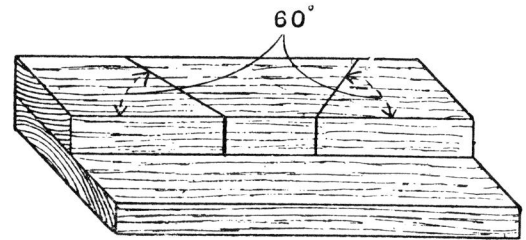

Fig. 41.—Block for Hexagonal Joints.

The table top is $\frac{3}{4}$ in. thick and 1 ft. 9 in. square outside, with the corners chamfered and a hollow cut in each side, as shown by Fig. 43, an alternative design for the top being shown in the half-plan, Fig. 44. The sides are fitted with strips of $\frac{5}{16}$-in. split bamboo, as illustrated by Fig. 45, and a strip of thin cane runs round the edge. The frame for the legs is 1 ft. $6\frac{3}{4}$ in. square at the bottom, and 1 ft. $0\frac{1}{2}$ in. square at the top, the distances being measured from the centres of the bamboos. The four legs are $1\frac{1}{2}$-in. canes, and are connected, at distances of $8\frac{1}{4}$ in. and 1 ft. $10\frac{1}{4}$in. from the bottom, by $1\frac{1}{2}$-in. rails about 1 ft. 5 in. and 1 ft. 2 in. long respectively. These rails are fitted with plugs and brads. The two strips B (Figs. 42 and 46), 1 ft.

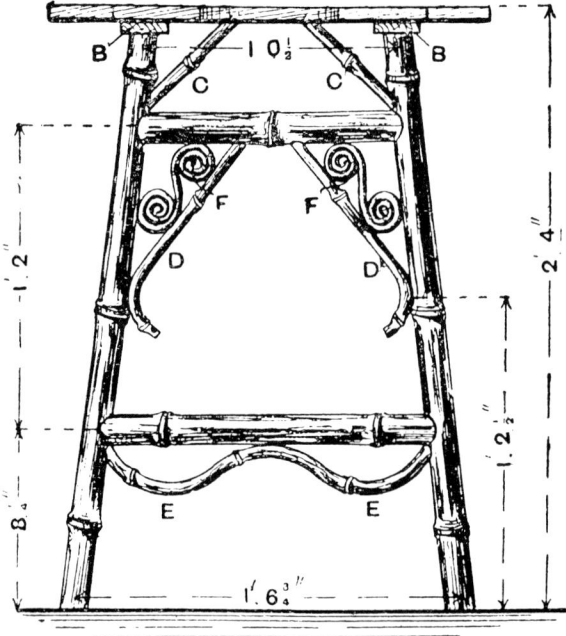

Fig. 42.—Bamboo Occasional Table.

3 in. long, 2 in. wide, and $\frac{1}{2}$ in. thick, have circular recesses into which the plugged ends of the tops of the legs are fixed. The legs are then screwed from above, as shown in Fig. 46, and the pieces B fixed to the top. Eight stays of $\frac{5}{8}$-in bamboo about $6\frac{1}{2}$ in. long are fitted in at c (Fig. 42), eight about 1 ft. long at D, and four about 1 ft. 8 in. long at E. Eight fillings of $\frac{1}{4}$-in. bamboo are fixed at F.

The table top can be of walnut, or it can be black enamelled on a wood foundation with gilt ornamen-

tal figures. Care must be taken that the holes are drilled before the nails are inserted to prevent the bamboo splitting. Fig. 47 is a horizontal section just above the lower rails, and shows the under shelf; this shelf is $\frac{1}{2}$ in. thick, and fixed as shown by Fig. 48; it should be of the same wood as the top.

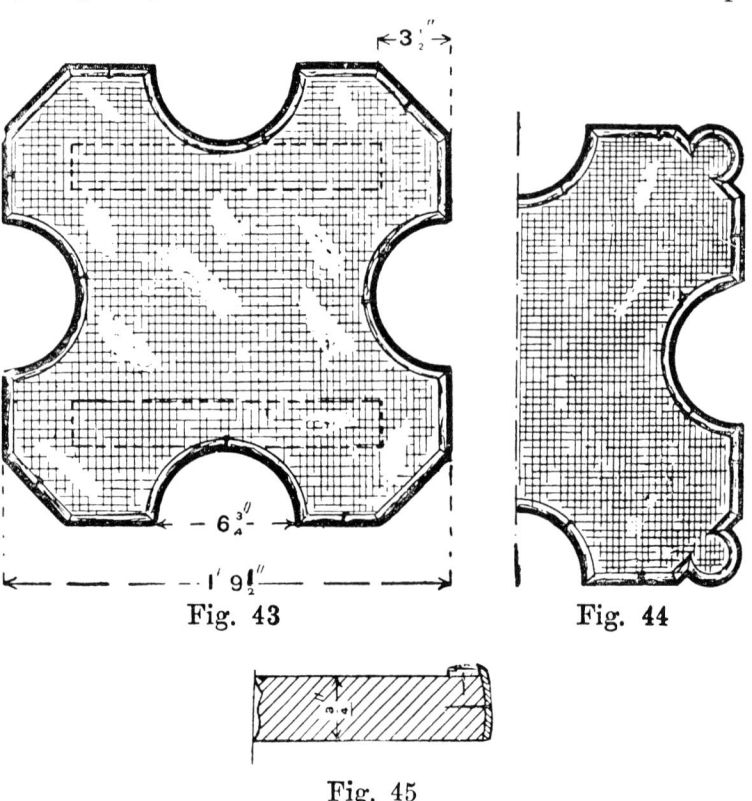

Fig. 43.   Fig. 44.

Fig. 45

Fig. 43.—Table Top.   Fig. 44.—Alternative Half-design for Table Top.   Fig. 45.—Section of Table Top Edge.

The ends of the rails and stays should be plugged before being fixed in position.

The construction of a four-flap bamboo tea table is shown by Fig. 49, p. 50. The movable shelves are of wood or lacquer, the top is of wood covered with Japanese matting or with a lacquer panel, whilst the under shelf is a lacquer panel. The design of tea table illustrated has become very popular. The table is 2 ft. 3 in. high. Select four 1¼-in. canes and bend out the toes and cut off to 26 in. long. In all such cases the canes should not be cut off to the precise length until the bending is done, as the bend cannot be made quite at the end of the cane. The top end of the legs must receive plugs 3 in. long well glued in.

Four cross-rails, 11½ in. long (1½ in. being allowed for fitting), should now be cut from 1¼-in. canes.

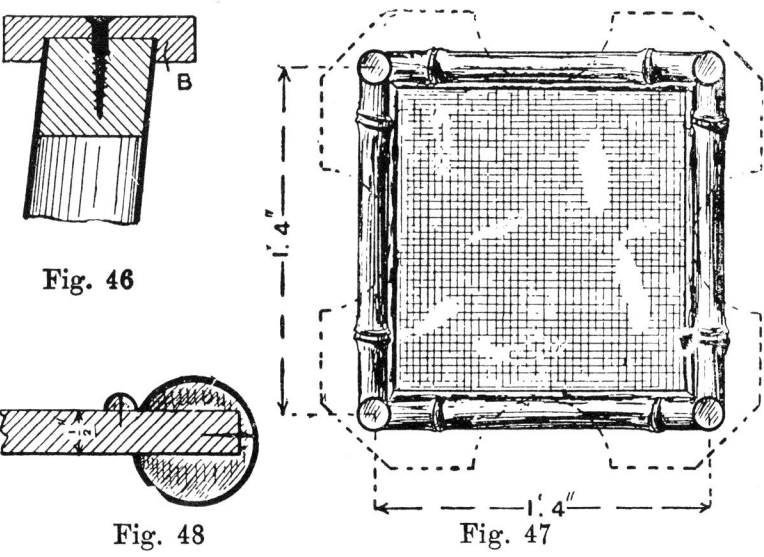

Fig. 46

Fig. 48   Fig. 47

Fig. 46.—Joint between Table Top and Leg. Fig. 47.—Section of Table showing Shelf. Fig. 48.—Section showing Shelf Joint.

The ends of these four rails must be hollowed and dowelled, or otherwise fitted to the four legs as described on pp. 34 and 35; care must be taken to finish all the rails to the same length. The four legs and the four rails will then be fitted together, and framed up as two flat sections.

The system of forming flat sections in bamboo work is to be recommended. In general, a section may consist of four rods, framed together to form

D

a square or oblong; these rods are fitted together, and the glue allowed to dry, before the different sections are united to form the completed article. Care must be taken to make the various flat sections perfectly symmetrical and alike, so that they will go

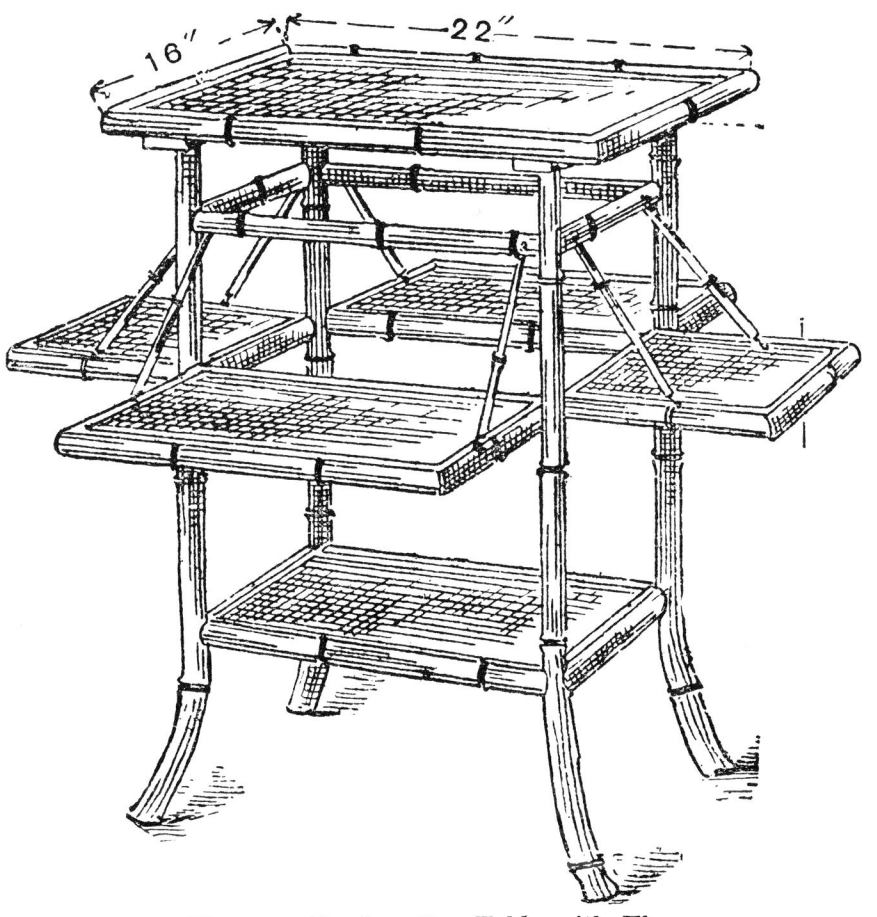

Fig. 49.—Bamboo Tea Table with Flaps.

together quite true. One of the best ways of testing a section is by measurement from point to point diagonally.

For the flat sections of the table in question, the canes with the largest bore should be used, and care must be taken to bore the legs for dowels, so that the bent toes will point outwards from the four corners of the table when it is put together. The large bore canes are chosen for the two sections, so that the dowels used for fastening them together may be as large as possible, and for this reason the holes drilled in the legs to receive them should be as near the size of the dowel as possible, so that little trimming down will be required. Glue, clamp up the sections, and leave a few hours until the glue is set. Now cut off four rails 15½ in. long (1½ in. is allowed for fitting). With these front rails the two sections will be framed together. The holes bored to take the dowels for these must be considerably smaller than those of the four side-rails; they should be as small as circumstances will allow, as these holes must cut into the dowels already glued in without dividing them; these second dowels should not go quite through the first ones.

The movable flaps may now be made and fitted; deal, ½-in. thick, planed up on one side, 9 in. by 9 in. for the end flaps, and 13 in. by 9 in. for the side flaps, is generally used for this purpose. The top of the table, 15 in. by 21 in., can be made from 1½ in. or ¾-in. deal, planed up on one side.

The Japanese matting for covering the top, lower shelf, and movable flaps, must be prepared for gluing by being roughened on the wrong side with sandpaper or the flat side of a rasp. The matting may now be cut to the required sizes, leaving a little margin for final trimming round the edges.

The prepared wood must then be coated well with hot glue, and the matting put on; air bubbles are rubbed out, and then it is weighted down and left a few hours to dry. When the glue is set the matting must be trimmed round the wood with a sharp knife, care being taken not to fray it at the edge. The edges of the top and shelf and flaps must now be beaded with split bamboo, mitred at the corners and fastened on with 1¼-in. panel pins

(the edging should stand slightly above the surface of the matting); an angle will thus be formed to receive a thin bead of white cane, which will fill up any imperfection there may be in the edges of the matting. The cane should be carefully mitred at the corners, and fastened down with ⅝-in. beading pins.

If, instead of covering the top with matting, the top is to be formed of a lacquer panel, cut a board the size of the lacquer about ½ in. thick, screwing two fillets across where the legs will come (see Fig. 50), cutting with a centre-bit four holes about halfway through, for the top of the legs to fit into; then fix it on the frame with glue and bamboo pins. Fix the lacquer panel on the top with a few screws inserted from the underside of the wood, taking care that the points do not come through; then edge round with the ¾-in. bamboo; mitre the corners and fix with bamboo pins into the wooden top, and finish off the top with an edging of split black beading cane. Similarly the lower shelf may be of lacquer fitted in between the traverses, secured in like manner with pins through the bamboo and edged with beading cane.

The flaps must now be attached to the table. Thick 2-in. wire nails must be driven into the two back corners of each flap, projecting ½ in. to form pins which will slide in slots cut in the sides of the legs for their reception. These slots must be 5 in. long, and commence ½ in. below the top cross-rails. To make them, first bore holes with a large bradawl, where the top and bottom of the slots should come, and clear out between these holes with a knife, or with a cutting gauge (Fig. 11, p. 25). The slot should be ⅛ in. wide when finished. The best material to use for the struts is ¼-in. rounded dowel wood, or, failing that, thick rattan cane. They must be 7 in. long, and the ends fitted with steel or brass screw-eyes. Two similar screw-eyes will be fixed in the top cross-rails of the table, and the struts attached by looping the eyes together. The other ends of the struts will be attached in a similar manner to the eyes screwed into the flaps; the exact position of these will have to be obtained by trial; they must be fixed so that the flaps hang perfectly level. If desired the struts may be fixed with screw eyes to the legs of the table instead of to the cross-rails; the choice is immaterial.

For fixing on the top, two battens, 2 in. wide by $\frac{5}{8}$ in. thick by 14 in. long, should now be fastened into the tops of the legs by 3-in. thick wire nails driven into the plugs, and to these the top must be attached with glue and $\frac{3}{4}$-in. screws.

The flaps, instead of being covered with matting,

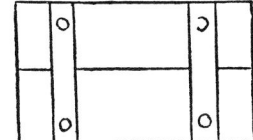

Fig. 50.—Underside of Tea Table **Top.**

may be of lacquer; this is mounted on thin wood edged with $\frac{3}{4}$-in. split bamboo and beading round the top. The flaps are just long enough to work easily between the legs. When not in use the flaps can be folded down flush with the legs by raising the pivot ends.

To finish the table, clean off superfluous glue and apply some good spirit varnish. The undersides of the top, shelf, and flaps should be stained. A pennyworth of vandyke brown and a pennyworth of ammonia in a pint of water make a good stain for this purpose.

A writing table is illustrated by Fig. 51. The most convenient measurements for the writing table would be: height (exclusive of outside railing) 2 ft. 6 in., depth 2 ft., and length 3 ft. 2 in.

Fig 51 shows the desk complete and finished; whilst Fig. 52 shows a skeleton of the top part, which consists of a simple tray, the side of which is cut for a drawer to be inserted. Two drawers would look as well as one, and would be equally easy to make. If two drawers are to be employed, runners, A A, Fig. 52, will be required.

The top may be of walnut wood, stained and polished, and the edges are rounded and polished and well finished-off. The bamboos round the sides of the desk will be required to be neatly fas-

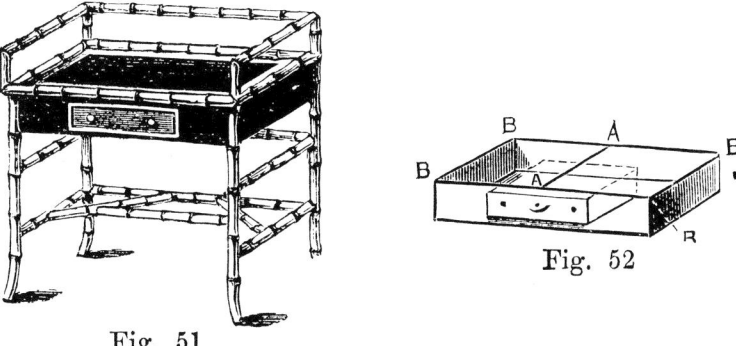

Fig. 51

Fig. 51.—Bamboo Writing Table. Fig. 52.—Tray and Drawer of Table.

tened, as also the rail; and this can be done by running small screws and nails under the sides of the canes.

A combined hall seat and table in bamboo is shown by Figs. 53 and 54; $1\frac{1}{2}$-in. canes are used in its construction. The two front feet should be toed out and cut off 25 in. long, and the back feet are of the same length, but straight. Four pieces, each 2 ft. 9 in. long, and four pieces, each 14 in. long, should be cut to form the rails; 3 in. of these lengths is allowed on each rail for chisel pointing, mortising, and fitting, thus making the inside distance between the front legs 2 ft. 6 in. At distances of 5 in. and 16 in. from the bottom bore the two front legs to receive the dowels, with which all the rails should be plugged. Then fit together as a flat section, repeating the operation with the two back legs and long rails, squaring and clamping with string, and glueing. While the sections set, proceed with the construction of the seat arms which are made from

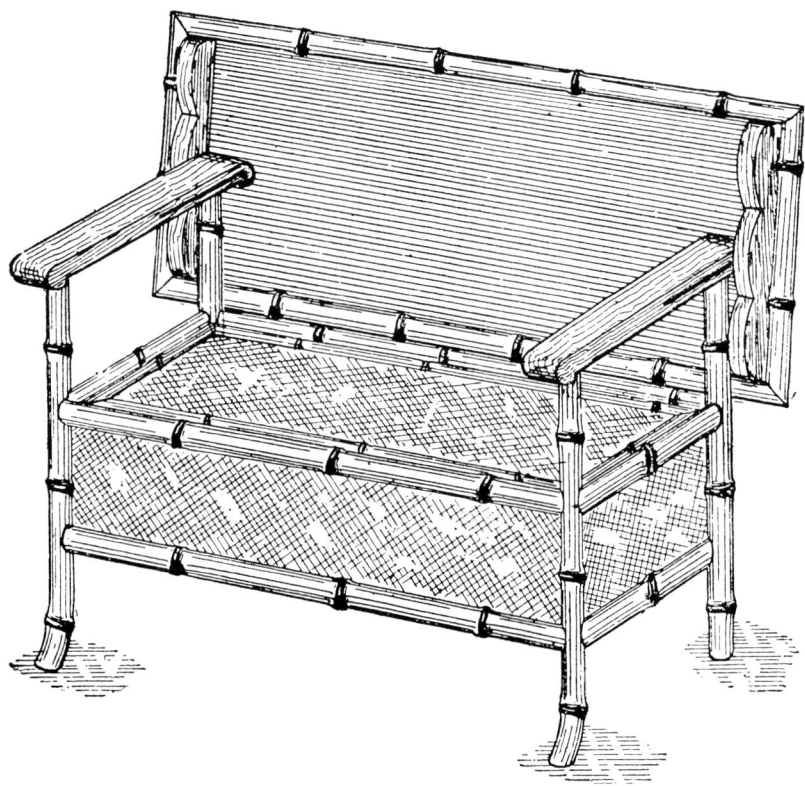

Fig. 53.—Combined Hall Seat and Table.

beech, 16 in. long, $2\frac{1}{2}$ in. across, and $1\frac{1}{2}$ in. thick. A narrow groove is cut through the arm from the centre to near the end to admit a bolt, as is shown by the thick lines on the arms, Fig. 53. The two pieces (Fig. 55) by which the table top is fixed to the arms must be 16 in. long and 1 in. thick. The table top is of $\frac{3}{4}$-in. deal, 34 in. long and 18 in. wide. One side should be planed, sandpapered, and

stained to form the back of the seat. The top should now be placed in the position it will occupy on the seat arms, with the supports shown at Fig. 55, and the places marked so that they can be screwed into the proper positions. It is better to screw through the top and into the support. A pencil passed through

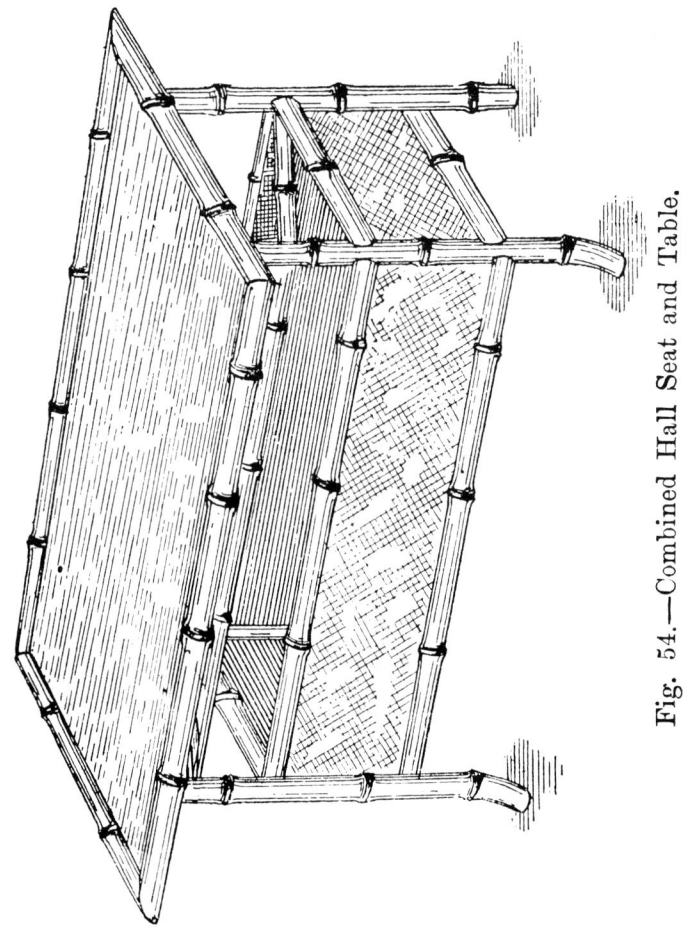

Fig. 54.—Combined Hall Seat and Table.

the groove at the centre will mark the position at which the hole is to be bored in the support to receive the bolt. The countersunk head of the bolt should be placed at the inside of the arm. The sides, ends, and bottom of the box should be prepared from $\frac{3}{4}$-in. deal; they are fixed in position by panel pins driven through holes bored in the legs and rails of the frame. One side of the wood should be planed to form the inside of the box. Japanese matting should now be cut for the sides of the box and the table top. This should be roughed with sandpaper or the flat side of a bamboo worker's rasp to afford a tight hold for the glue. A piece of 1-in. wood forms the seat, one side being planed up and the other side matted. The seat should be slipped round with ½-in. split bamboo, and a small

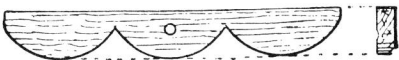

Fig. 55.—Table Top Support.

brass pull added for lifting purposes. The seat should be hinged on two thick wire pins, in the same manner as are the doors of the combined cupboard and bookcase described on p. 108. A piece of wood should be screwed along the front and sides of the inside of the box to form a rest for the front of the seat. To convert the table into a seat, push the table-top along by the front edge until the bolts reach the end of the slot, when the top will tip up and form a back. The whole should be completed by the application of a coat of spirit varnish, recipes for which are given on p. 39.

CHAPTER IV.

BAMBOO CHAIRS AND SEATS.

BAMBOO chairs require to be constructed with the maximum of strength, because the strains to which they are subject are far greater than those endured by tables, fancy stands, and similar pieces of furniture. The joints, being the weakest parts, must be made very carefully; and the materials used must be of the best.

Fig. 56 shows a bamboo chair complete. The bending of the legs, made from $1\frac{1}{4}$-in. or $1\frac{1}{2}$-in canes, is the first work. Those at the front are simply "toed out," as in making a table, and cut off 16 in. long. The leg and back must now be bent as in Fig. 57. This figure should be drawn out full size on paper and the bamboo bent and applied to the drawing time after time until the correct shape is obtained; in the workshop a templet leg is always kept. Three lengths each of 13 in. should now be cut, 2 in. being allowed for fitting; they form the rails for the back of the chair. These rails should be hollowed, dowelled, glued, and cramped up, and the section put aside to set. A piece of $1\frac{1}{4}$-in. cane 14 in. long (2 in. being allowed for fitting) must now be cut off to form the rail for the front legs. Previous to fitting, the two legs should be dowelled at the top. The rail may be fitted and dowelled, and to form a section a piece of wood may be fastened temporarily across the top by driving two nails through the wood and into the dowelled legs; see Fig. 58. As the nails must be taken out before the seat is fixed, do not drive them right home. The filling of the chair back is made from wood 6 in. by 4 in., covered with matting, and made as described on pp. 82 and 83. This centre is a design of common occurrence in bamboo work. Two pieces of 1¼-in. cane, each 13 in. long (2 in. for fitting), should also be prepared for the two side rails and a piece of ¾-in. wood cut out for the seat; see Fig. 59. The two back corners should be gouged out to fit the round of the back legs. The two sections should now be fitted

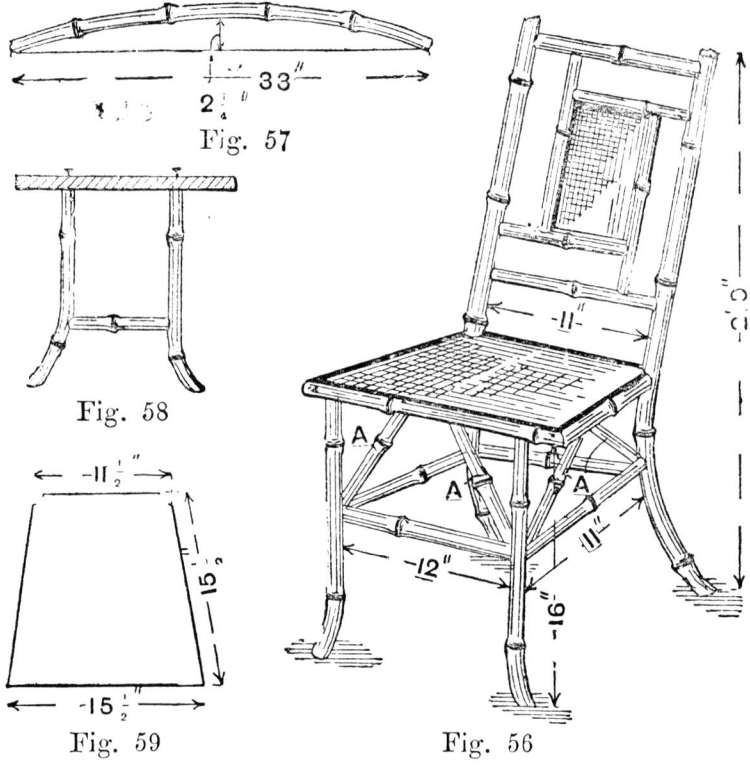

Fig. 57

Fig. 58

Fig. 59

Fig. 56

Fig. 56.—Bamboo Chair. Fig. 57.—Chair Leg and Back.
Fig. 58.—Front Chair Section. Fig. 59.—Chair Seat.

and joined together. A hole should be made through each of the legs with a small shell bit 16¼ in. from the bottom, and the back of the seat should be attached to the legs by screws. The top should be attached to the front legs by screwing through into the dowelled legs, the temporary piece of wood having previously been removed.

While the frame is setting, eight stays (A, Fig. 56) may be prepared, one end of each being fitted to the legs and the other to the bottom of the seat; fix them with glue and fine beading pins. Also fix the plaque or filling for the back. The seat should be covered with Japanese matting, unless it has been decided to upholster it, and finished with a slipping of split bamboo, and an inside bead of white

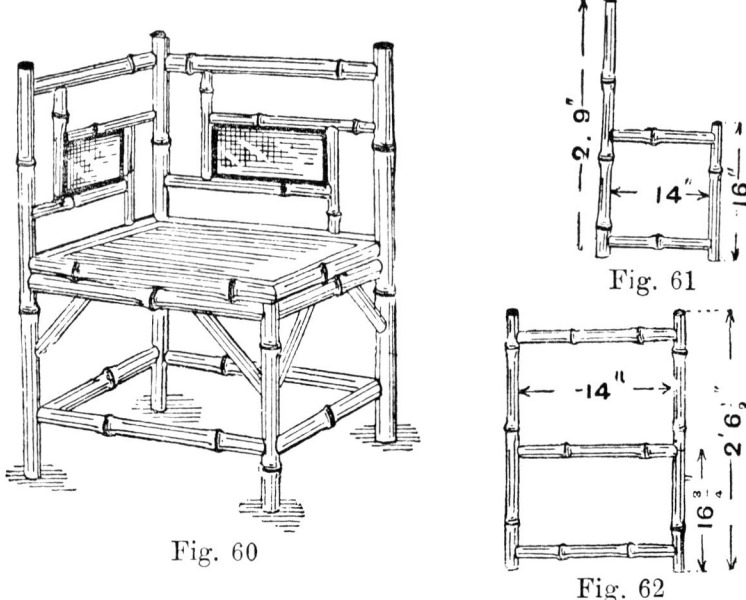

Fig. 60

Fig. 61

Fig. 62

Fig. 60. — Bamboo Corner Seat. Figs. 61 and 62. — End Sections for Corner Seat.

cane, as is described for the tea table on p. 52. The tops should be dowelled and fitted with terminals, and, except for cleaning off and varnishing, the chair is complete.

A corner seat ready framed up is shown by Fig. 60. From 1¼-in. or 1½-in. canes cut three pieces, each 2 ft. 9 in. long, and one piece 18 in. long, to form the four legs, and eight pieces, each 16 in. long (2 in. for fitting), to form the rails. Fit up to Figs. 61 and 62, and taking care to place the middle rail in Fig. 62 ¾ in. higher than the top rail in Fig. 61, as the seat in front rests upon the front rail, while it is screwed into position through the back centre rails. While the two sections are setting make the plaques or fillings and the seat, this being 14 in. square. Fit and dowel the other rails, and when the sections are dry frame the whole up, taking care that the two back centre rails are ¾ in. higher than the two front rails. When the frame is dry, fit on the eight stays, fix in the plaques, and

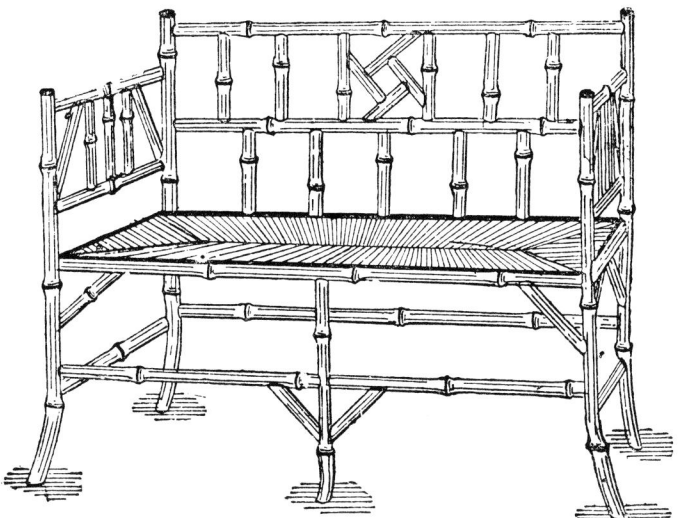

Fig. 63.—Bamboo Settee.

fasten on the bottom. Plug the tops of the uprights, put on terminals, clean off, and varnish.

Fig. 63 illustrates a settee, and Figs. 64 and 65 show its front and back sections. Make up these from 1¼-in. or 1½-in. canes, first bending out the toes for the three front legs. The eight side rails may be 15 in. long (2 in. for fitting). When the sections are dry, fit up and put the frame together. Fig. 63 shows a rush seat, but, if preferred, either plain or upholstered matting can be substituted. The seat is made to fit between the four rails, and is

screwed in position. Strong stays should be used all round the settee. Finish by cleaning off glue, etc., and then coat with white shellac spirit varnish.

A chair or settee for two persons is illustrated

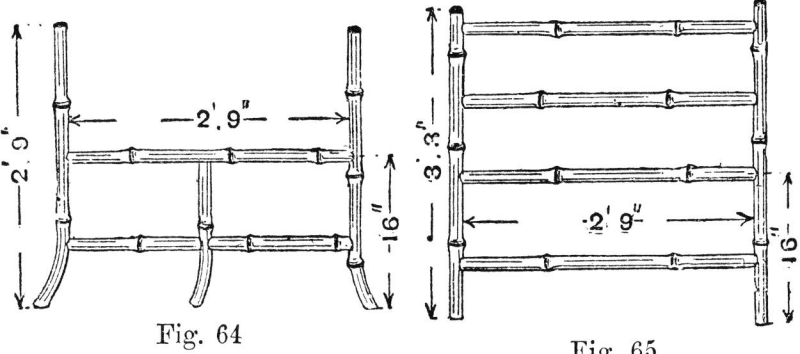

Fig. 64   Fig. 65

Fig. 64.—Front Section for Settee.   Fig. 65.—Back Section for Settee.

by Fig. 66; the seat and back are composed of flat strips of bamboo let into slots, forming a sort of spring cushion. The strips of flat bamboo are obtained from between the joints of very large canes,

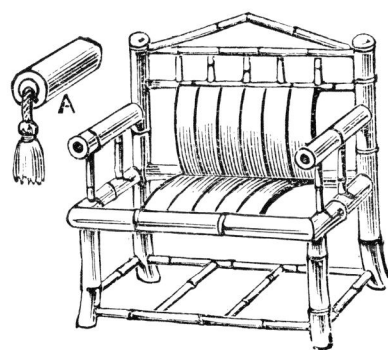

Fig. 66.—Bamboo Double Chair or Settee.

after well steaming the canes are hammered flat with a mallet on the rough side. Strips can seldom be obtained wider than 2 in. Fig. 67 shows back portion of the chair, Fig. 68 showing the underside of the seat. Care must be taken that the chair is firmly fixed together, or it will creak if a heavy per-

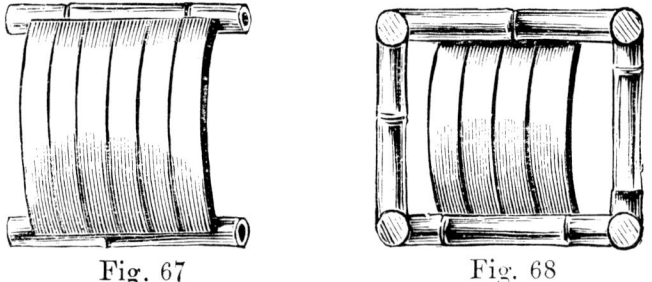

Fig. 67   Fig. 68

Fig. 67.—Settee Back.   Fig. 68.—Under side of Settee Seat.

son uses it. The ends of the arms look well if finished off with turned boxwood plugs with tassels

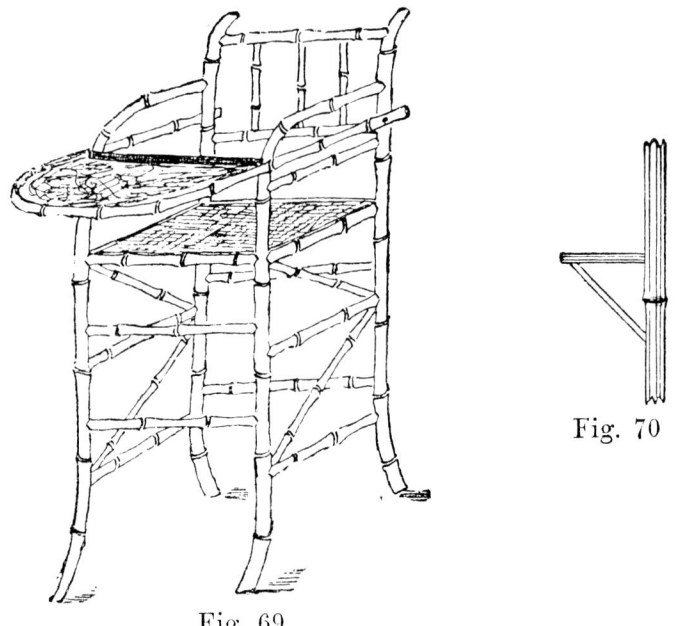

Fig. 69

Fig. 70

Fig. 69.—Child's High Chair.   Fig. 70.—Foot-rest Support.

hanging from them (see A, Fig. 66). The legs should be bent outwards at the lower ends to add strength, lightness, and comfort.

A design for a child's high chair, with tray, is shown by Fig. 69, p. 63. Make the front legs and arms in one length; this gives additional strength, and there is no difficulty in bending the bamboo. The four legs should be well splayed out at the bottom to avoid the risk of the child tilting the chair either backwards or forwards. Every joint should be dowelled, glued, and pinned, and such pieces as the three uprights in the back should be let directly into the frame.

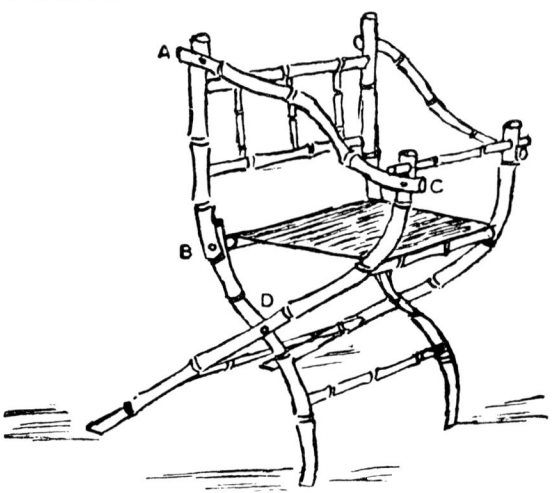

Fig. 71.—Baby's Folding Chair.

The tray is best formed from an oblong Japanese tray, and can be cut to shape, leaving a ledge on the square side. Support the tray on small pegs let into the front arms. For the sides of the tray bend a piece of 1-in. bamboo to the required shape and hinge it to the back legs with bamboo pegs or neat bolts and nuts. The chair is 3 ft. high over all; the seat is 2 ft. from the floor, 11 in. wide by 12 in. deep, and is cut out of a plain deal and covered with Japanese matting, the edges being finished off with split beading cane. There is ample room for a loose cushion if required.

Should a foot-rest be wanted, support it on

brackets let into the front legs. For each bracket will be required two ½-in. canes, one 4 in. long and the other about 6 in. long. The shorter one is dowelled into the chair leg at right angles; the longer one is dowelled into the leg about 3½ in. below the other one at an angle of about 45°, its free end being joined to the free end of the shorter cane (see Fig. 70, p. 63). On these brackets, the foot board, if one is required, may rest. The risk of the chair tilting forward is increased by the foot-

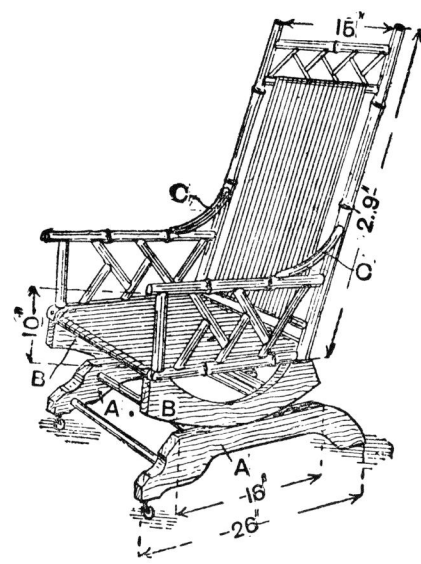

Fig. 72.—Bamboo Rocking Chair.

rests which are not desirable additions. The legs should be weighted with lead as described on p. 44.

A baby's folding chair, having a carpet seat, may be made after the style of Fig. 71. The joints, A to C and A to B, must be of such a length that when the trestle folds up the back falls backwards and lies parallel with the straight legs. A, B, C, D are the four points on which the chair folds, and, with the exception of joint D, the bamboos can be plugged, and so long as the holes are made without splitting, this will be found strong enough, as the bars, or tra-

E

verses, on which the seat is fastened, take part of the strain. Use small bolts and nuts with a washer at each side for the joints, 1¼-in. bamboo for the trestle part, and 1-in. for arms and bars.

The rocking chair shown by Fig. 72, p. 65, has beech rockers which are made in two parts from 1¾-in. wood. The two pieces A for the base can be joined together either with four birch or bamboo rails, 15 in. long when finished, and the front should have casters. The top rockers B are 17 in. long, and form the base on which the sides of the chair will be built; 1¼-in. or 1½-in. canes should be used for this work. The two uprights should be fixed to the

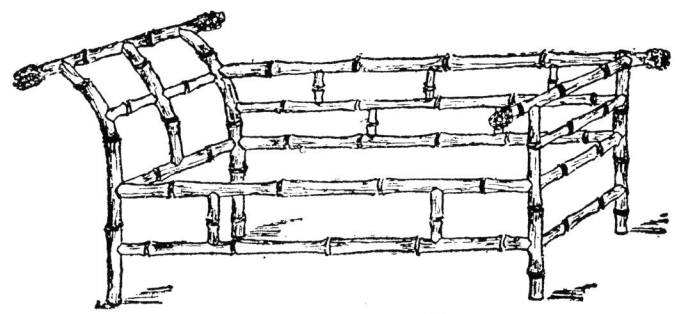

Fig. 73.—Bamboo Couch.

rocker with hardwood dowels, fitted into holes bored in the rocker at one end and into the hollow tube of the upright at the other end. These dowels must be a perfect fit, as upon them the stability of the chair greatly depends. The two rails for the side and arm of the chair should be fitted, filled, and, after the uprights have been glued and fixed, screwed into position with round-headed screws. A bamboo cane should be bent as at C, and fixed with nails as a stay between the arm and back of the chair. The herringbone filling (see p. 99) between the arm and bottom rail now is fixed. The pieces for this work, after being fixed, should be filled with dowels so as to strengthen the arms. The two sections when set should be joined together with the six cross rails, which should be 15 in. long when finished. The rails on which the upholstering is fastened are filled right through with deal dowels to give a hold for the nails. Add the herringbone filling to the back, and after the upholstering is done, the chair will be ready for fixing to the base with two special rocking-chair springs.

The framework of a bamboo couch is shown by Fig. 73. Great strength is necessary, and so every joint must be dowelled. The couch is shown having arms with root ends, which add much to the finish and cost but little, the bent arm having a root at both ends, one being, of course, a false one plugged on. The legs should be of $1\frac{3}{8}$-in. or $1\frac{1}{2}$-in. bamboo, and care must be taken in bending them at the top end, as it is difficult to bend such thick cane without injuring it. The seat consists of $\frac{3}{4}$-in. deal joined to the required width, fitted within the frame, and secured with 3-in. wire pins through the bamboo, and further with bamboo stays running from the legs to underneath the seat. Intermediate work, such as the pieces between the main framework, need not be dowelled, but simply plugged and rasped out to fit, and secured with glue and pins. Rasp the surface to be glued, otherwise the glue will not hold. In the event of fixed upholstering being required, rough wood frames will do instead of the filling-in work to fit within the main work, lining them with good canvas and webbing. Saddle-bags or velvet hide much that should otherwise be the charm of bamboo furniture, and a better effect is obtained by making any upholstery detachable; thus for the couch, use a loose seat and several cushions. The couch should be from 4 ft. 6 in. to 6 ft. long, according to requirements, and from 21 in. to 24 in. back to front. Finish off with spirit varnish, or, better still, by French polishing.

CHAPTER V.

BAMBOO BEDROOM FURNITURE.

THERE is no limit to the number of articles of furniture that can be constructed of bamboo; and it is not at all impossible to furnish any particular room in a house with suites of furniture made almost entirely with this material. This chapter will describe the construction of the more important furniture found generally in the bedroom or dressing room.

A bamboo bedstead may be about 6 ft. 6 in. long by

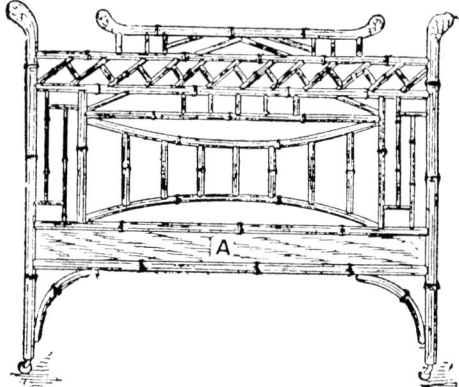

Fig. 74.—Foot of Bamboo Bedstead.

3 ft. wide. Fig. 74 shows the foot of such a bedstead. Figs. 75 and 76 are alternative designs for the head. The framework of each of these sections must be made from stout $1\frac{3}{4}$-in. to 2-in. canes, and great care must be taken in making the joints and seeing that the dowels are a good fit. A (Figs. 74 to 76) is a piece of beech 7 in. wide and $1\frac{1}{4}$ in. thick. This must be fitted in position 1 ft. above the ground before the filling work is commenced, and should be securely fastened with round-headed screws passed through the legs and cross rails into the wood. The strength of the bedstead in a great

measure depends on the firmness of this piece of wood, as on it are fastened the angles by which the head and foot are stretched. The filling work next can be proceeded with, care being taken that every joint is strong and a perfect fit. Fig. 75 shows a design suitable for an upholstered back, 7 ft. 9 in. high; if preferred, similar work to that shown in

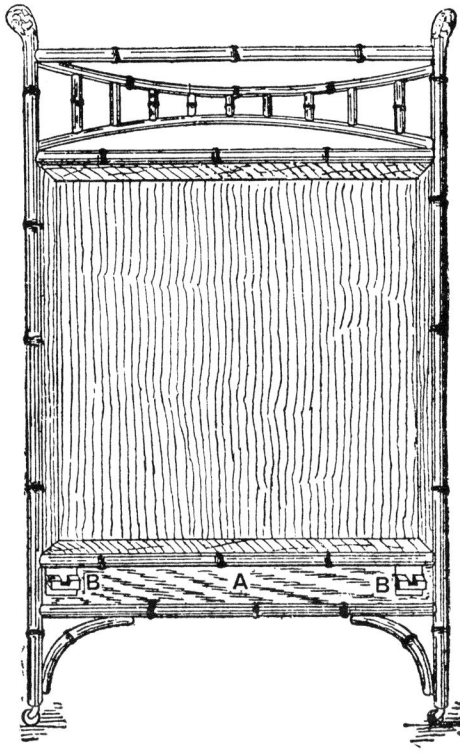

Fig. 75.—Head of Bamboo Bedstead.

Fig. 76 can be used. For the bedstead bottom, iron fittings, similar to those used for wood bedsteads, are advised. Fig. 77 is a sketch of the iron angle, and the position in which the angles are placed is indicated sufficiently by B, Fig. 75. The iron angles are securely fastened to the wood with screws, and the stretchers and laths are attached in the usual manner.

Fig. 78 shows a child's bamboo cot, which will be found easy of construction, light, and strong. As illustrated, the corners of cot and the stand are made with root-end canes, but brass knobs could be substituted for the roots if preferred. The cot itself has a length of 3 ft., is 16 in. wide at top, tapering to 12 in. wide at bottom, and 15 in. deep. Webbing is not required for the bottom, as bamboo traverses or cross-pieces answer the same purpose and help to

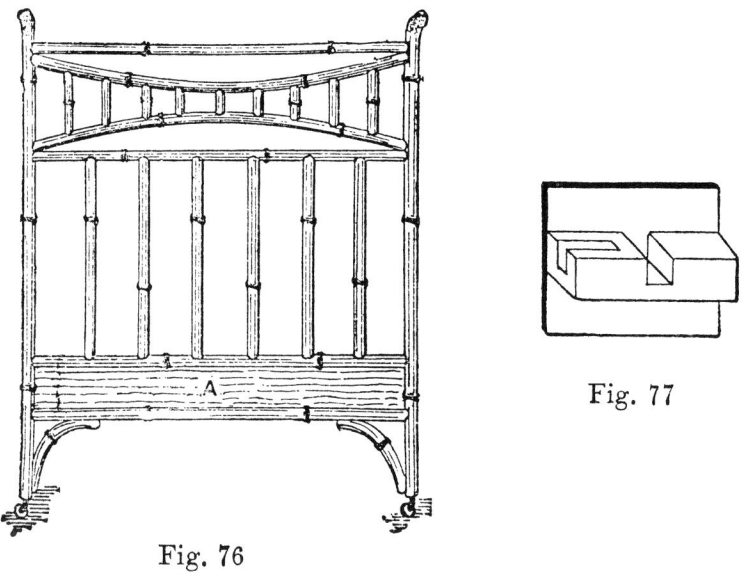

Fig. 76

Fig. 77

Fig. 76.—Head of Bamboo Bedstead. Fig. 77.—Iron Angle for Bamboo Bedstead.

keep the cot rigid. The corner posts of the cot extend a few inches above and below the top and bottom bars, in order that they can be properly dowelled into the former. The framework of the cot—that is the corner uprights, rails, and intermediate uprights—should be of $1\frac{1}{4}$-in. bamboo, either brown or tortoise-shell, whilst the filling-in work should be of $\frac{3}{4}$-in. or 1 in. bamboo. The centre upright for the stand is of $1\frac{1}{2}$-in. bamboo, the top being 2 ft. 9 in. from the floor. The legs ($1\frac{1}{4}$ in.

in diameter) are bent, and then fixed as shown to the uprights, and further secured with a rail near the bottom, the cot being swung on the stand by means of a bolt at each end. At the head is a curtain rod of ¾-in. bamboo, which is fastened inside, not outside, the top end. Take care to make good joints, and the result will be very satisfactory. The pattern of the sides and ends may be varied to suit individual taste. When the cot is not wanted to swing, fix it to the stand by means of brass hooks and eyes.

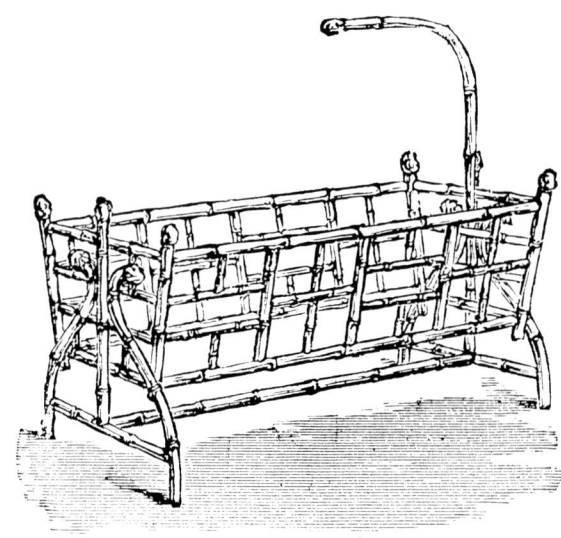

Fig. 78.—Child's Bamboo Cot.

A child's bamboo cot of a different design is illustrated in part by Fig. 79, p. 73. For making this cot, select four canes not less than 1½ in. in diameter for the corner posts; cut these to the length required and fix a stout plug in each end. For the frame of the bed, use 1-in. canes. Bore holes in the four corner posts after the fashion of a mortise-and-tenon-joint, those for the ends to be higher than those at the sides, and the canes can be fixed in these and held with a fine, long screw. Webbing can be used for the bottom, and if this is used the simplest way

is to make a good loop at each end and slip them over the canes before fixing i nthe posts. A better way, however, is to use a piece of stout canvas the size of the crib and lace it to the sides. Bamboo being rather slight, will have to be put together very accurately, and at least two stretchers should be used to keep the frame rigid. The top rail can be fixed in the same manner as the bottom, and from these a lattice work of smaller canes can easily be constructed. A good plan is to have a kind of under-rail to keep the legs firm; Fig. 79 will help to make everything clear. The dimensions are best fixed as circumstances require. The four posts can be finished off with knobs, and casters may be fixed on the bottom end; or an equally good plan is to have the bottom plugs turned a little larger, and projecting beyond the end about 2 in. As bamboo has many crevices it is well to fill up any small spaces in the joints with a mixture of plaster-of-Paris, brown sienna, and glue mixed up into paste form; when dry this will prevent insects hiding in out-of-the-way cavities; or any of the fillings mentioned on p. 38 can be employed.

From the illustration Fig. 80, p. 75, the dressing table about to be described may appear to be an ambitious piece of furniture. But attention to the instructions given below should result in a very creditable job. Fig. 80 shows the dressing-table complete. Of course, the measurements may be altered at pleasure, but those given will be found suitable for ordinary use. First get two 1¼-in. bamboos about 6 ft. long; these are to be bent slightly at the bottom. Cut off two pieces 32 in. long for the two front uprights, A A. Get two more bamboos of the same diameter and cut off two pieces 45 in. long for the back uprights, B B

Proceed to make the back and front frames. First mortise six rails 33½ in. long out of 1¼-in. bamboo; these must be roughed inside at the ends with a round rasp in order to make the glue adhere. Plug both ends with dowels about 6 in. long, leaving about 1 in. projecting ; do not as yet glue in the plugs. With a $\frac{5}{8}$-in. centre-bit bore three holes in each upright at 1 in., $6\frac{1}{4}$ in., and 29 in. respectively, measuring from the top of the front uprights. The point of the bit enters 1 in. from the top of each upright.

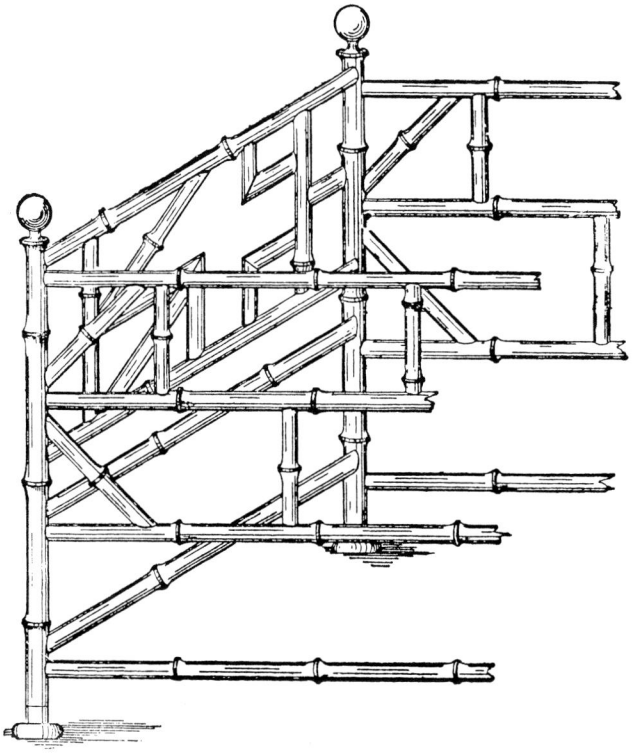

Fig. 79.—Another Design for Bamboo Cot.

Take the six rails, pull out the plugs and shave these to fit in the holes bored. Fit the frame together to see that all joints are neat, and then take to pieces again for gluing up. Have the glue hot and rather thick, and get the frame together as quickly as possible. Tighten up with strings passed round and twisted tight with pegs (see Fig. 10, p. 24, and Fig. 163 p. 145). Put aside for the glue to set. Mortise two

pieces of $1\frac{1}{4}$-in. bamboo $33\frac{1}{2}$ in. long for the two uprights, C C. These are to be plugged at both ends and then dowelled on to the top rail of the back frame, leaving $18\frac{1}{2}$ in. between. Make three rails to fit in, leaving a space of 3 in. between the top rail D and the second rail E, and $24\frac{1}{2}$ in. between E and F ; plug these rails, and insert long panel pins, boring first with a fine bradawl to avoid splitting the bamboo. Bend a piece of 1-in. cane, G, to the required shape ; fit this, and dowel on to the two uprights C, C, leaving it to hang over for about 2 in. on each side (see G, Fig. 80). Five pieces of $\frac{1}{2}$-in. bamboo each 5 in. long, have to be fitted in between the top rail and the bent top bamboo, and must be rasped to fit. Four $\frac{7}{8}$-in. bamboo canes, mortised to $6\frac{1}{4}$ in., are for the two sides H H (Fig. 80), and are placed at a distance of 3 in. apart, measuring 1 in. from the top of upright. The small slanting pieces are of $\frac{1}{2}$-in. bamboo 4 in. long, and are mortised to fit, glued and nailed on with fine 1-in. pins. Bend two $\frac{3}{4}$-in. bamboos with roots to the required shape for J J, and spindle them on to the two uprights C C with pieces of $\frac{1}{2}$-in. bamboo 4 in. long. Mortise six $1\frac{1}{4}$-in. bamboo canes, 16 in. long, for the side rails M ; plug in the same way as were the front and back rails, and with a $\frac{1}{2}$-in. centre-bit bore holes in two frames ; fit, and then glue up the same way as before. Square up the whole stand and let it remain for a day or so for the glue to set quite hard.

The frame for the mirror may be made whilst the stand is lying aside. It is of 1-in. bamboo or of ordinary wood, as may be preferred. The inside measurement is 22 in. by 16 in., and the corners have to be strongly and carefully mitred. Nail round some fine beading cane to form a rebate for the glass to rest on ; put in the silvered glass and back with thin board. Put this aside, and commence to fit the top and side panels. The top panels are of spruce or pine covered with matting or Japanese

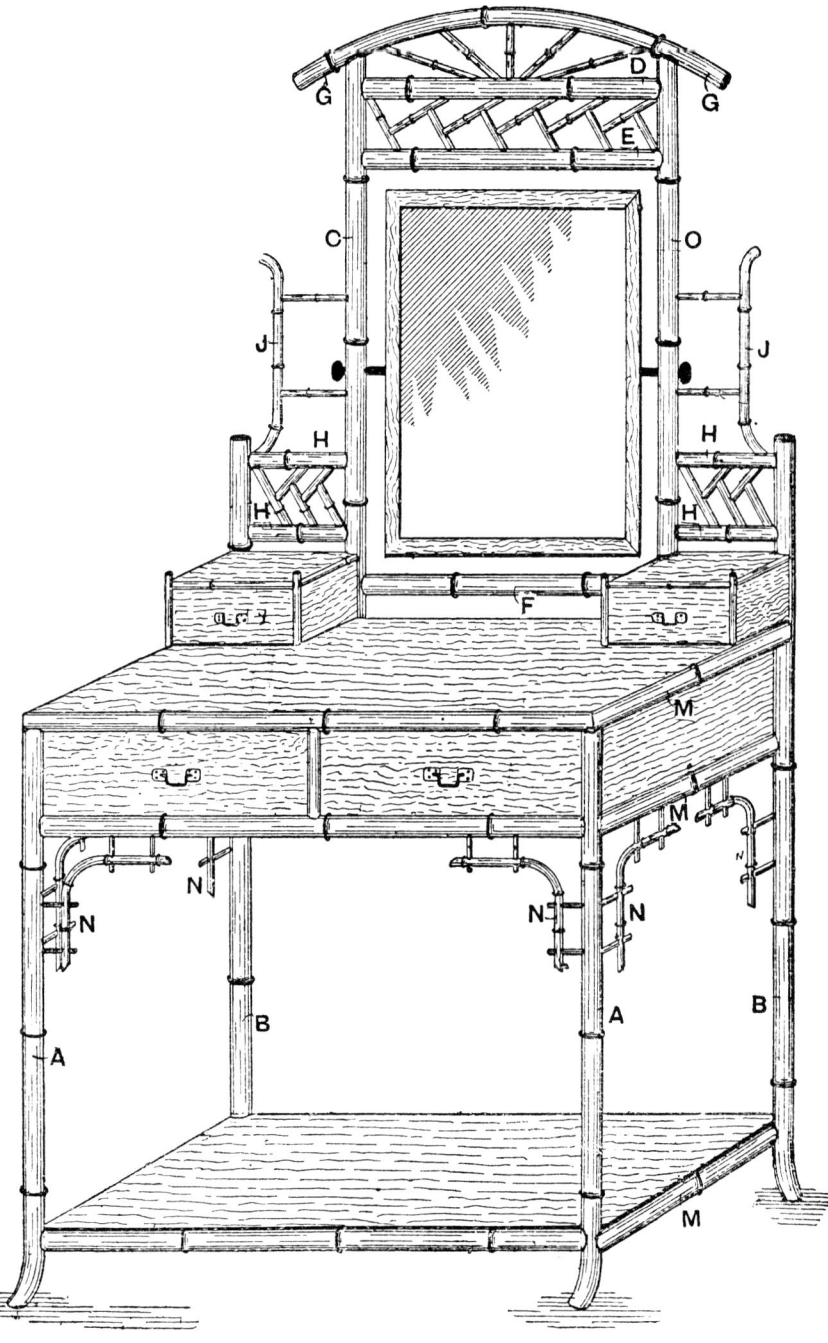

Fig. 80.—Bamboo Dressing Table.

paper. The matting is glued on as is described on p. 51. Nail beading cane round the edges. The side panels are of lacquer work, and the back can be a piece of spruce stained brown.

Now take four pieces of $\frac{1}{2}$-in. bamboo $4\frac{1}{2}$ in. long; these have to be spindled into the table-top $6\frac{1}{4}$ in. apart and 4 in. from the back. Fit a rail in between each, $\frac{1}{2}$ in. from the top, and a rail on either side; plug and nail with fine pins. Get some $\frac{1}{2}$-in. bamboos and bend to the required shape for the six curved pieces N (Fig. 80), which are spindled on to the frame with thin pieces of cane 5 in. long.

Fit the lacquer panels on top and at sides, and secure with pins. Fit the panels between the rails, then bore right through the rails with a fine brad-awl and secure with 2-in. panel pins. Make two small drawers to fit; the front of each drawer should be a piece of lacquer. Make also the two large drawers, which have lacquer fronts; it will be an improvement if the panels are beaded round with cane. Now fit panels in under the table, and cover with matting or Japanese paper, in the same way as was the table-top. The mirror frame swings on a pair of brass tighteners which are fitted on the two uprights. Four brass handles for the drawers are put on with small brass screws.

The dressing-table is now complete, and requires only a coat or two of hard white varnish to finish it; this should be applied in a rather warm room. It would perhaps be an improvement to use lacquer instead of matting or paper for the table-top, but this would add to the expense, and matting looks very well, and is very durable when used with ordinary care.

A bamboo washstand to match the bamboo dressing-table just described is illustrated by Fig. 81. This design should not present difficulties to anyone sufficiently skilful to make the table above mentioned. The uprights A A and B B should be got out first ; the former are 32 in. long, and the latter $40\frac{3}{4}$ in. The front ones are bent slightly at the bottom, and this should be done before they are cut to size. Plug the ends and with a $\frac{5}{8}$-in. centre-bit bore holes in a line at 1 in., $6\frac{1}{4}$ in., and 29 in., measuring from the

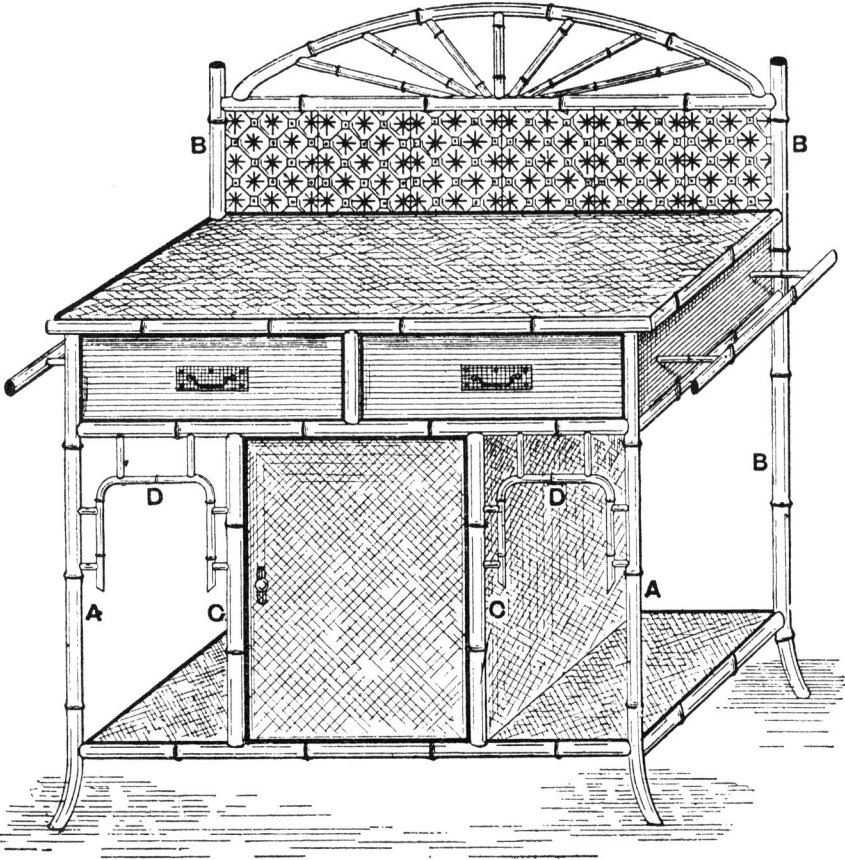

Fig. 81.—Bamboo Washstand.

top of front uprights A A. An additional hole is bored in the back ones B B $2\frac{1}{8}$ in. from the top. Now put these aside and get seven pieces of $1\frac{1}{4}$-in. diameter bamboo $37\frac{1}{2}$ in. long and mortise to 36 in. ; these are for the long rails. Rough them inside at the ends with a round rasp, and plug with dowels at least 6 in. long, leaving 1 in. projecting ; shave

the end of pegs to fit tightly in the holes bored in the uprights. Then fit the two frames together, taking care that all joints fit neatly.

Now take to pieces for gluing up ; this process resembles the putting together of the dressing-table as explained on pp. 73-76. When this is done put the framework aside and get six pieces of bamboo $1\frac{1}{4}$ in. diameter ; these must be mortised to 16 in. In cutting up bamboo for rails, $1\frac{1}{2}$ in. is allowed for the waste entailed by mortising. The six rails are for the sides ; rasp and plug, then take the two frames and bore holes with a $\frac{1}{2}$-in. bit to receive the plugs ; fit in the same way as before, and then glue and square the whole frame. The distance apart between the two top rails at the back is 6 in., and in this space half a dozen 6-in. square tiles are fitted. Thin beading cane is nailed round first to form a rebate, the tiles are then put in, and cane is nailed round at the back to keep the tiles in position. The bottom panel, which now is fitted in, is made of deal $\frac{5}{8}$ in. thick planed on both sides. Secure this with 2-in. panel pins, which are driven through the rails, boring first with a fine bradawl. Now make four rails $27\frac{3}{4}$ in. long to form a frame for the cupboard, as shown at C C. These are plugged and secured with long pins ; fit panels in sides and at the back in the same way as in the case of the bottom panel. The two sides of the latter and the cupboard should be covered with matting or Japanese paper.

Make a rail to fit in between the two rails at the top of front, then make the drawers and fit them ; the fronts of the drawers should be pieces of Japanese lacquer. The door for the cupboard is made of a piece of deal, the front being covered with matting, and split bamboo mitred at the corners is nailed round the edge. A small brass cupboard turn and two brass hinges are fitted on the door.

The table top is of deal, and 1 in. is allowed to hang over on each side except at the back ; the top is attached with 2-in. screws which enter from the back of uprights B B, and two are driven from the top of table into the plugs in the uprights A A (Fig. 81). Cover with matting; or, if a more elaborate job is required, a marble top is very suitable; this is easily fixed with screws. If matting is used, bamboo 1 in. in diameter is nailed round the edge, the corners being mitred. Bend some $\frac{1}{2}$-in. cane for the fancy work, D D, and spindle on with pieces of thin cane

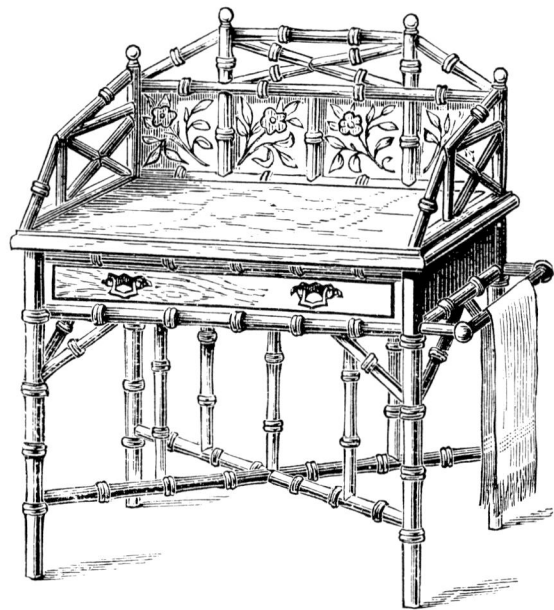

Fig. 82.—Bamboo Washstand.

3 in. long. The bent piece for the top is made out of 1-in. diameter cane, and the small slanting pieces are made out of $\frac{1}{2}$-in. cane. The centre one should be 5 in. long; the others must be cut to fit, as their lengths greatly depend on the way the top bamboo has been bent. Cut two pieces of 1-in. bamboo 16 in. long for the two towel rails, and spindle them on to the frame with 4-in. pieces of $\frac{1}{2}$-in. bamboo.

All the woodwork of the washstand including the inside of cupboard, in which a shelf can be fixed if

desired, should be stained walnut colour. Finish the washstand by varnishing it in a warm room.

Another design for a bamboo washstand is given in Fig. 82, p. 79. The table portion is well supported by the four legs and by five additional uprights dowelled into the diagonal cross-rails.

The swing glass with a bamboo frame, illustrated by Fig. 83, will accommodate a mirror measuring 21 in. by 15 in. It is made as follows:—First make of 1-in. bamboo a frame with mitred joints to fit the glass, the bamboos being first plugged and then glued and pinned together. Rasp the knots down level on the inside, and fix an edging of split beading cane round the frame to form a rebate for the glass. Back it with thin wood or millboard and secure it also with beading cane. The glass, with frame, will measure 23 in. by 17 in. so should be swung 12 in. from the bottom. Allow $3\frac{1}{2}$ in. clear space between bottom of frame and drawer top, $2\frac{1}{2}$ in. for depth of drawers, and $1\frac{1}{2}$ in. below; this will make the side supports $19\frac{1}{2}$ in. high to centre of top rail (see Fig. 84), and 22 in. in all; cut the uprights to 23 in. to allow for the small bend at the top and the angle at which they are fixed, they being 3 in. apart at A and 9 in. at C (Fig. 84). The uprights, as well as the cross-pieces B and C, are of $\frac{3}{4}$-in. bamboo; but the top cross-piece A is of 1-in. bamboo. The cross-pieces must be dowelled into the uprights. If the top-piece A has not a knot the plug will go right through, and thus will give additional strength. The space between B and C is filled in with a piece of Japanese lacquer, secured with wire pins through the bamboo, and edged with split beading cane. The bend at the top of the uprights is made in the usual manner. The cross-pieces between A and B are of $\frac{1}{2}$-in. bamboo plugged and rasped out to fit, then glued and pinned to the uprights. To determine the distance between the two uprights, leave a clear space of $\frac{1}{2}$ in. each side of the looking-glass, and cut the bamboos that form the two uprights and make the case for the drawers accordingly; a piece divides the drawers in front. Having fixed the uprights fit in the top and bottom of drawer case; the bottom need only be of common deal, but the top should be of lacquer, in character with the sides and back. The drawer fronts also are of lacquer, with fancy brass handles.

The glass is swung on bamboo pivots, which are

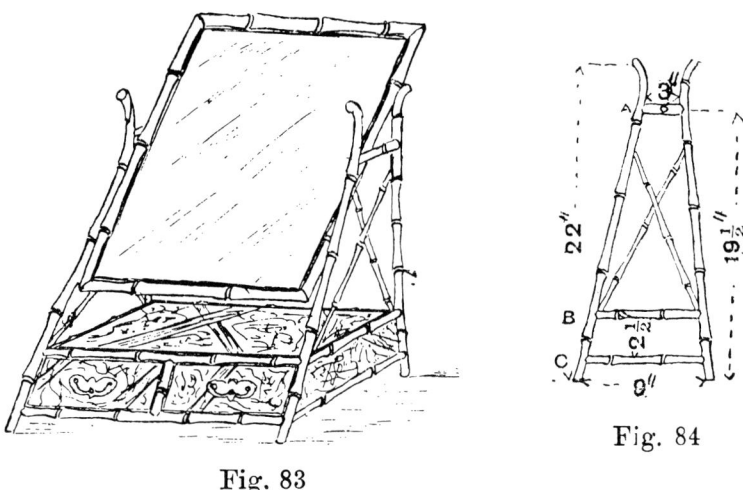

Fig. 83

Fig. 83.—Toilet Mirror with Bamboo Frame. Fig. 84.—Side of Mirror Frame.

made thus: cut out two pieces of $\frac{3}{8}$-in. bamboo about 3 in. long from between the knots and plug them right through. Then cut a $\frac{3}{8}$-in. hole with a centre-bit through the cross-pieces A, and also in the looking-glass frame 12 in. from the bottom end, but not right through. The pivots should fit firmly in the cross-pieces and be secured with a wire pin, and also be fairly tight in the mirror frame, so that the glass will remain stationary at any angle at which it is put. Small brass knobs screwed in the ends of the pivots are a nice finish.

CHAPTER VI.

BAMBOO HALL RACKS AND STANDS.

A VERY simple rack or rail for hats can be made from 1-in. bamboo canes, as shown in Fig. 85. Cut off two lengths, each 44 in., for the top and bottom of the rack; then cut five lengths, each 9 in., for the uprights. Shape the ends of these uprights as in Fig. 86, A, with the rasp, so that they will fit on to the rods along the top and bottom of the rack; in Fig. 86, A is the upright and B the top rod. Fit a wooden dowel 2 in. or 3 in. long into A; each length when rasped should be 7 in. Mark off spaces in the

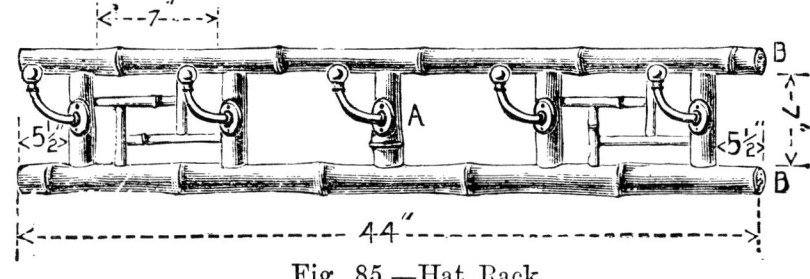

Fig. 85.—Hat Rack.

long rods, taking care to allow 1 in. for the thickness of each upright, and next bore holes into the rods B B (Fig. 85), where marked for the uprights. It is better to bore the holes slightly smaller than the dowel, which can then be reduced to fit, because if the holes are too large the joints will be loose and thus reduce the strength of the rack. The dowels must then be fixed in the drilled holes in B with hot glue, and gently hammered home. Before gluing, fit the dowels into the drilled holes to ensure good joints.

The construction of the ornamental part of the hat rail is shown by Fig. 87. A shows the dowel fitted, but not driven home. The ornamental part should be made in ½-in. bamboo, and fixed into A and B B (Fig. 85) by holes bored with a small centre-bit, and fitted in before the whole is clamped together.

It should be observed, in cutting off the lengths for the top and bottom rails, that the knots in the bamboos come between the uprights. Glue and clamp up; fasten the whole together with fine French nails or screws, taking care always to bore holes for them or the cane will split. The ends can be finished with turned hardwood or bone terminals, and the pegs may be brass or rooted bamboo, according to fancy.

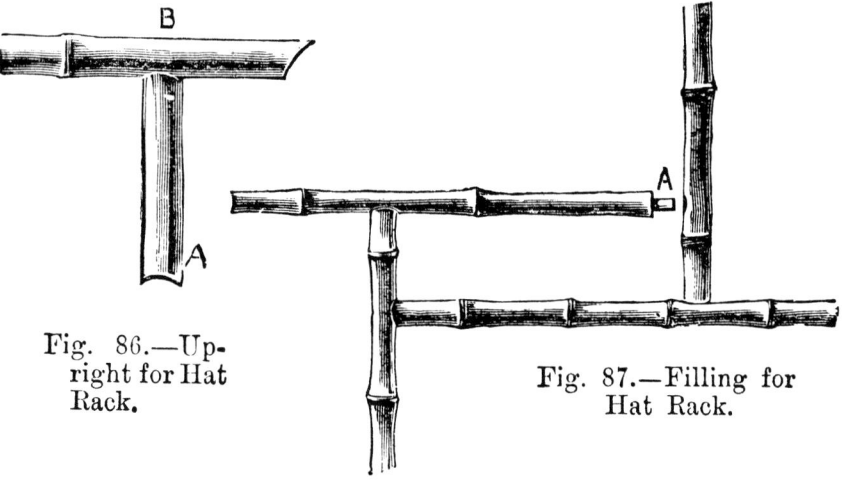

Fig. 86.—Upright for Hat Rack.

Fig. 87.—Filling for Hat Rack.

An umbrella stand may be made in bamboo to a very simple design as illustrated by Fig. 88, p. 84.

Four sticks, 1 in. thick, will be required, and the size of the stand is as follows: The four uprights, 2 ft. 6 in. long; six rails or traverses for front and back, 15 in. long; six side pieces, 8 in. long; two pieces at the bottom to rest the pan on, 8 in. long; a centre piece at the top, 8 in. long; and, finally, four little stays, 4 in. long. Plug both ends of the uprights, and, 1½ in. from each end, cut a hole with a ⅝-in. centre-bit, and a third one 4½ in. from the bottom end. Rasp out the ends of the six cross-pieces, to fit against the uprights and then plug each end,

leaving the plug protruding ¾ in. This should fit tight in the holes of the uprights, and be secured there with hot glue and a bamboo pin (see Fig. 89).

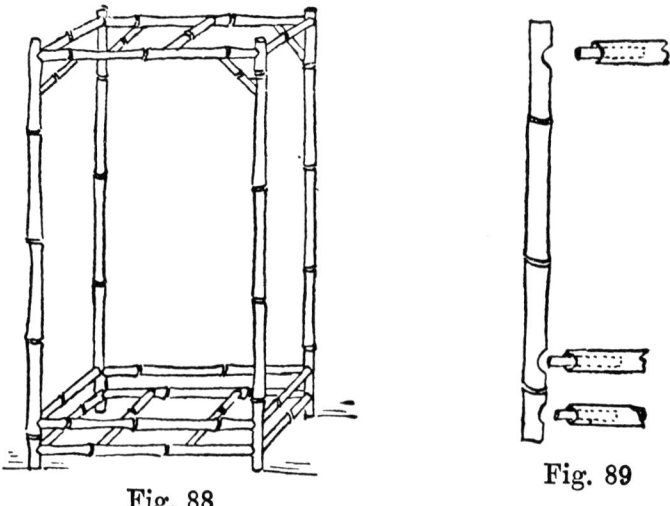

Fig. 88.

Fig. 89

Fig. 88.—Umbrella Stand. Fig. 89.—Joints for Umbrella Stand.

Fix the parts together, and bind them with string until the glue is quite dry. Plug each end of the six side pieces, and rasp the ends to shape, as before.

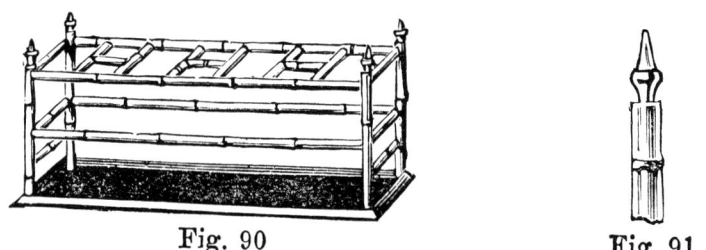

Fig. 90.

Fig. 91

Fig. 90.—Umbrella Stand. Fig. 91.—Terminal of Umbrella Stand.

They are glued to the uprights and further secured from the other side with a 2-in. bamboo pin; previous to gluing, the bamboo must be roughened. Before fixing the side pieces the two bottom pieces and the centre piece must be dowelled, as before, after which the whole framework can be put together and left to dry. Lastly, the four angle stays

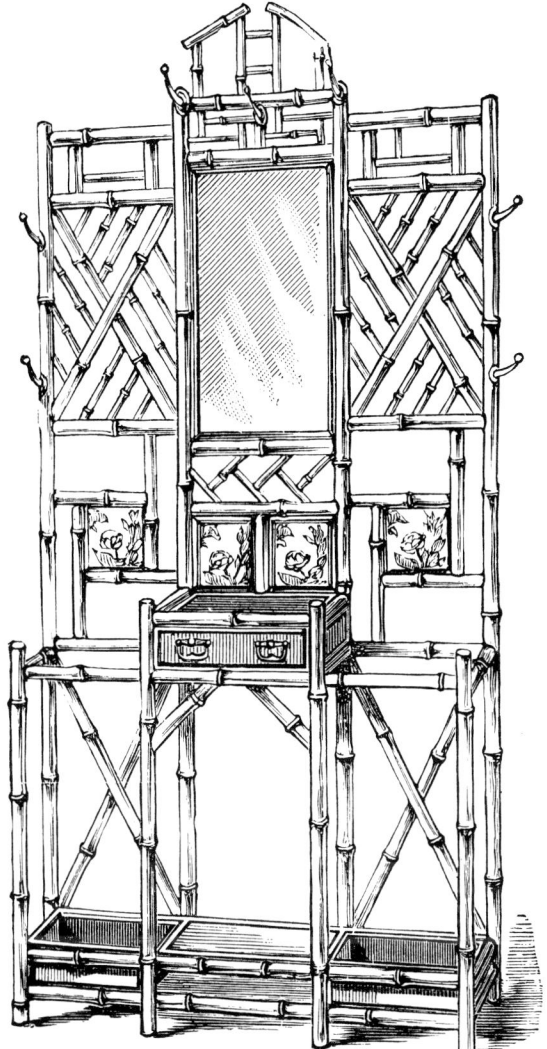

Fig. 92.—Hat and Umbrella Stand.

must be fixed on with glue and pins. A wooden button or terminal fixed on each upright will complete the construction of the stand, though, of course, a pan to receive the rain water drippings

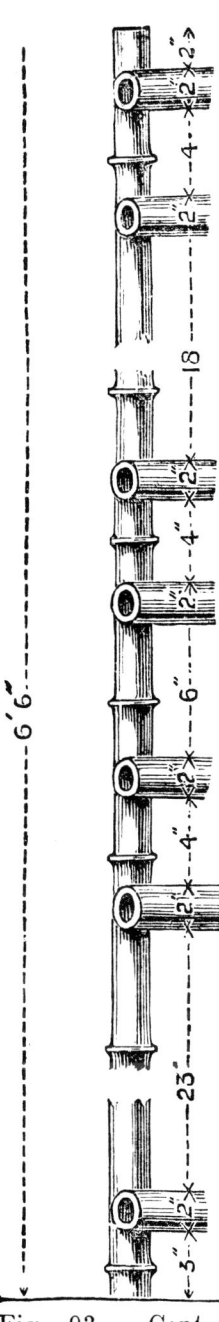

Fig. 93. — Centre Upright of Umbrella Stand.

from the umbrellas will be required. Clean off all superfluous glue, and give the stand a coat of varnish.

The umbrella stand (Fig. 90) p. 84, is similar to the last, except that the bottom is of wood with a wood edging round to form a well, in which should be let a brass or copper tray. The uprights are let into holes bored in the base. Fig. 91, p. 84, is an enlarged view of one of the terminals.

A more ambitious piece of furniture is shown by Fig. 92, p. 85. The hat and umbrella stand there illustrated may have the following principal dimensions: Extreme height, 7 ft. 6 in.; width, 3 ft. 6 in. Height of bottom portion, 28 in.; width between uprights, 12 in. Height of centre uprights, 6 ft. 6 in.; side uprights, 6 ft. 3 in.; depth of stand, 13 in. Size of mirror, 12 in. by 18 in.

Two $1\frac{1}{4}$-in. canes, each 6 ft. 6 in. long, will form the centre uprights. Cut seven canes 14 in. long (which, when rasped, should be 12 in.) and mark off the canes as in Fig. 93; allow 2 in. for each joint. Hollow the ends to fit on to the uprights, and cut dowels to fit into the ends of the canes; the dowels should project about $1\frac{1}{4}$ in. With brace and bit cut holes in the marked places in the uprights to receive the ends of the dowels; fit together loose, to see if all the joints are good. If all right, fix together with hot glue; also bore holes through the uprights, and fasten with wire nails or screws. If screws are used, countersink the heads. The whole should be clamped together until the glue has set thoroughly; for a clamp, use a string twisted as described on pp. 23 and 24. Cut two canes, each 6 ft. 3 in. long, and mark off as shown in Fig. 94. Cut ten canes, each 14 in. long, and fit to centre as described above; fit each part together separately, taking care not to get askew. The crossbars at the bottom should now be fitted, the ends being plugged with dowels, and nailed in their places with thin wire nails. Now fit together the panel to receive the tile or plaque, rasping the bamboo to fit; put in on the slant, and work to the proper position, taking care to keep the place for the tile or plaque square.

Fig. 30, p. 36, shows the dowelling of the diagonal pieces of the fancy filling. A dowel is put right through one of the rods and the two pieces fitted on; the other pieces are then rasped and fitted into their places with glue and small nails, care being

Fig. 94. — Side Upright of Umbrella Stand.

taken to keep them parallel with the centre cross. The tiles and glass are fastened in securely by nailing on pieces of split cane. The knots in the bamboo

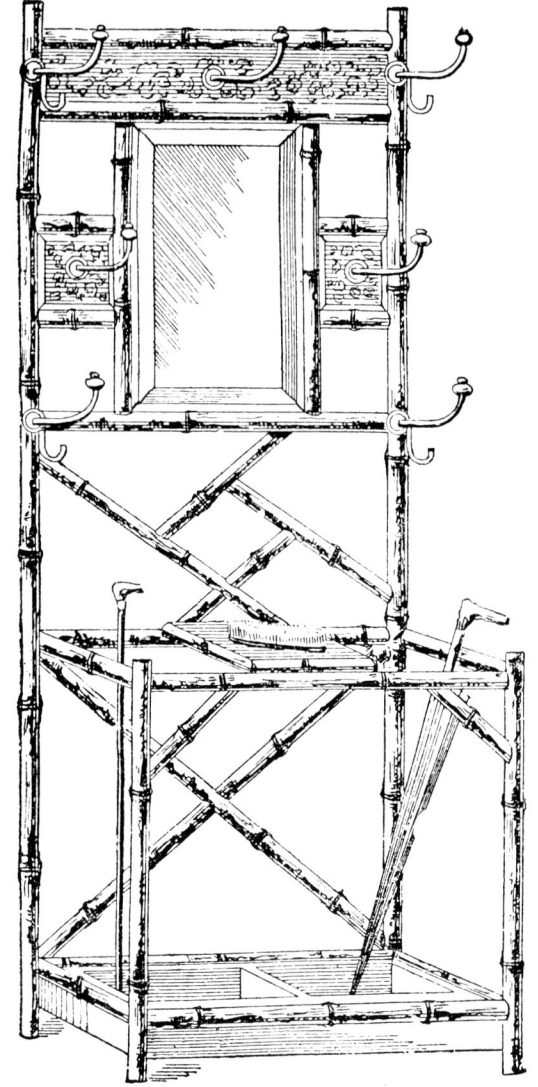

Fig. 95.—Hat and Umbrella Stand.

should first be rasped level, so that the tiles will fit well. Two pieces of wood should be let into the bamboo at the back of the glass by cutting mortise holes (as shown in Fig. 3, p. 20). Proceed to make the front part by cutting two canes, each 30 in.

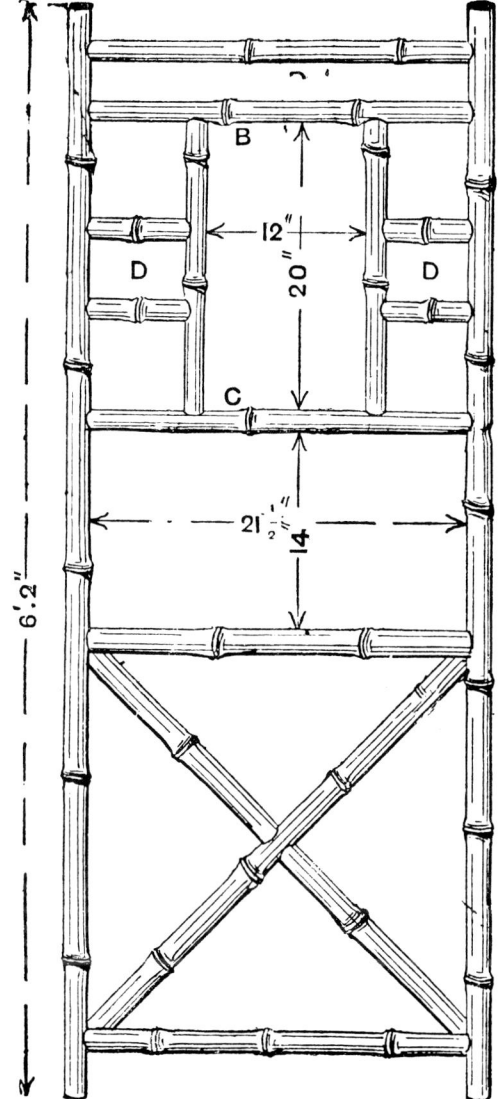

Fig. 96.—Back Section of Umbrella Stand.

long, and two 36 in. long ; six 14 in. long, to rasp to 12 in., and eight each 11 in. long, to rasp to 9 in.

Make the centre part by dowelling the centre

bottom stretchers ; glue up and clamp, and fit on the two sides. To make the fastening between centre and side stretchers very firm, put a screw through the back, so that it will go well into the dowel. Make and fit the drawer and supports, and fix together the front and back, using screws to make the whole firm. The sides, top, and front of the drawer and of shelf can be wood, plain or covered with Japanese matting, or may be lacquered plaques. Two japanned

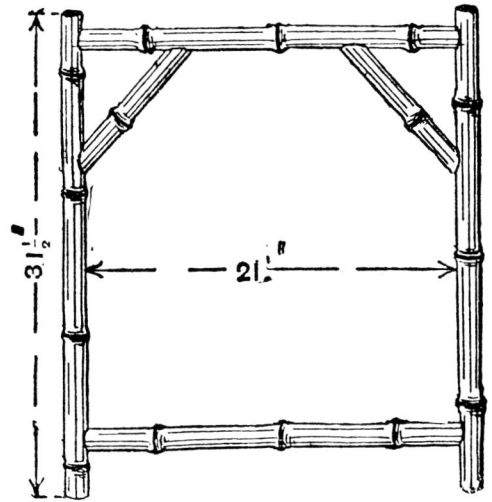

Fig. 97.—Front Section of Umbrella Stand.

trays will be required for the umbrellas. Either root bamboo or brass hat pegs can be used.

For the uprights in the bamboo hat and umbrella stand shown complete by Fig. 95, p. 88, 1¼-in. or 1½-in. canes should be used, and slightly smaller ones for the cross rails. Cut them to the lengths marked on Fig. 96, p. 89, allowing an extra 2 in. for the cross rails for hollowing and fitting. The mirror is 20 in. by 12 in., but it can be made longer by altering the position of the rails B and C (Fig. 96, p. 89). Fig. 97 shows the front. The four connecting rails measure 10½ in. when hollowed. The spaces marked D (Fig. 96) are filled in with wood covered with Japanese leather paper. The brush tray is made of a piece of $\frac{3}{4}$-in. deal covered with leather paper, and slipped with split cane. The tin pan at the bottom of the umbrella stand should have a lip at each end to keep it in place.

The hat-and-umbrella stand shown by Fig. 98 is

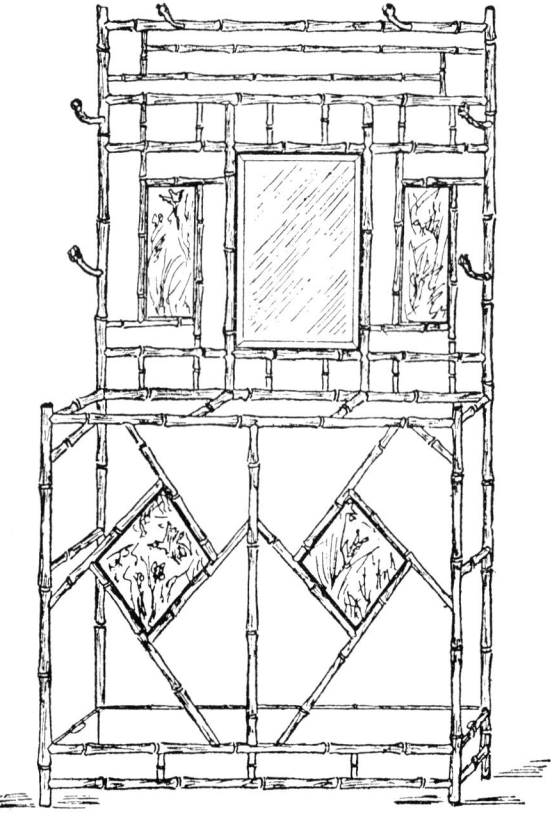

Fig. 98.—Hat and Umbrella Stand.

6 ft. high and 3 ft. wide. The bottom portion which holds the umbrellas is 2 ft. 9 in. high, and is fitted with a loose zinc pan, supported on traverses. The framework should be of $1\frac{1}{4}$-in. bamboo, the inner parts of 1-in., and the short spindles of $\frac{3}{4}$-in., let directly into the framework. The mirror measures 18 in. by 12 in.

CHAPTER VII.

BAMBOO MUSIC RACKS.

THE racks illustrated and described in this chapter are for the reception of sheet music, newspapers, magazines, etc.

A typical design is shown by Fig. 99, and for it four 1-in. and two $\frac{5}{8}$-in. canes will be required. From the 1-in. canes four lengths should be bent or toed out and cut off 20 in. long. Four pieces, each 16 in. long, for the four rails should now be cut off, also from the 1-in. canes, chisel-pointed, mortised (or hollowed) with the rasp, and fitted to their places. Holes should then be bored in the legs to receive the dowels, and the two sides framed up as described in previous chapters. While these sides, or sections, are setting, the two ornamental fillings should be made from $\frac{5}{8}$-in. cane. Four pieces of 1-in. bamboo, each 9 in. long ($1\frac{1}{2}$ in. is allowed for fitting), should be prepared to form the cross rails which are to join the two sections together. When the sections are set, holes should be bored to receive the dowels of the cross rails, and the whole then joined together. The two uprights for the partition are fitted to the bottom cross rail, and the top cross rail and upright are half jointed where they cross. The rail which carries the handle is mortised and dowelled at each end and fastened into position with two round-headed screws. The handle is made from $\frac{5}{8}$ in. cane, bent as shown, and fastened to the centre rail with round-headed screws. The rails which form the division of the partition, as also the three cross rails forming the bottom, are made from $\frac{5}{8}$-in. cane mortised at the ends and fixed into position with beading pins. A diagonal stay, not shown in the illustration, may be added to the central framework.

A design much on the lines of the last one is given by Fig. 100. The detailed letter references should make the construction of the other rack more intelligible. The rack illustrated by Fig. 100 may be made from ¾-in. canes. The four corner posts each 19 in. long, are slightly bent out at the bottom to form the feet. The posts are connected by three rails A, B, C, back and front, each 15¾ in. long, and at the sides by rails D and E (Fig. 100) each 9 in. long. There are also three cross rails running from front

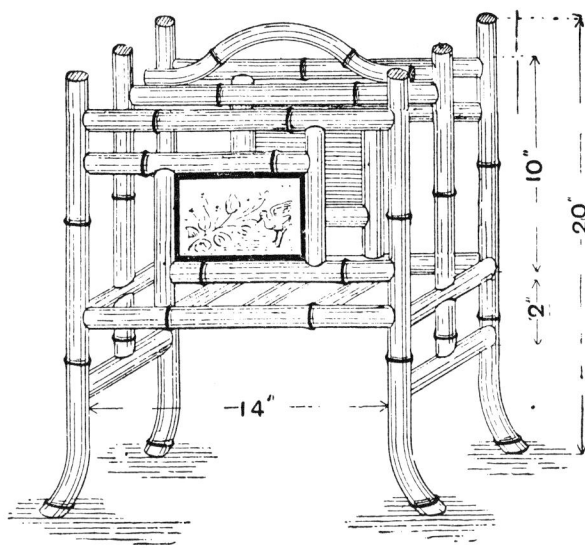

Fig. 99.—Two-Division Music Rack.

to back connecting the rail A. The rail E and the upright F (the latter being 13½ in. long) are halved where they cross. Between the centre uprights F is a rail G 15¾ in. long, to which the handle H, of ⅜-in. cane, is fastened. Running from the rail G are two ½-in. canes K, each about 19½ in. long, pinned together where they cross, and fixed underneath the rail D. An inclined rail J runs from B to C, the lower end being 1½ in. away from the corner post and the upper end, 5½ in. away. Another cane L (Fig. 100), 9 in. long, inclined in the opposite direction, meets the

rail J about 3½ in. from the top, and in the triangular opening thus formed panels are fixed. The dotted lines indicate how the cane L might be fixed if a variation in the design is desired. In this case the rail B would terminate where it met L. The centre of rail A is 6½ in., and the centre of B 9½ in., from the

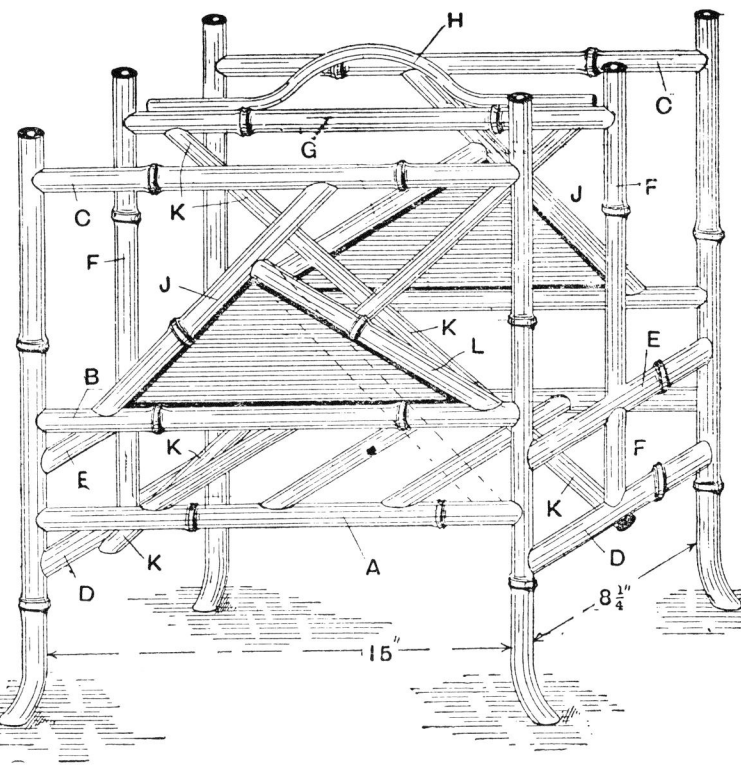

Fig. 100.—Two-Division Music Rack.

ground, and the distance between centres of D and E is 3¼ in.

A bamboo rack with three divisions is shown by Fig. 101 ; it can be made of ¾-in. or thinner bamboo. A useful size would be 15 in. high by 15 in. long, the divisions being 3 in. apart, and the four uprights or legs slightly bent outwards both at the top and bottom. Fig. 102 is an end view of the rack ; the two divisions are dowelled into the lower traverse whilst the upper division forms part of the bottom for the rack, being in a line with the bottom traverse of the sides. Fig. 103 shows one of the two partitions, and on the top traverse is a piece either of black or white beading-cane to form a handle. There

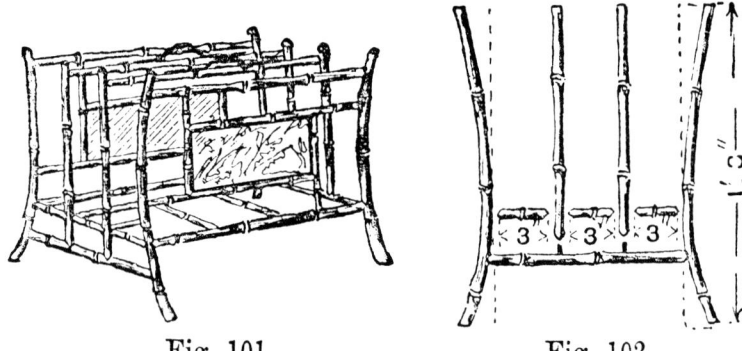

Fig. 101   Fig. 102

Fig. 101.—Three-division Music Rack. Fig. 102.—End View of Rack.

are also two cross traverses dowelled into the bottom traverses of the sides to form the bottom of the rack. The sides are filled in as shown by Fig. 101, the centre panel consisting of a piece of lacquer fixed into the bamboo framework with split beading-cane.

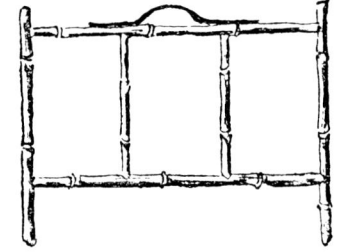

Fig. 103.—Partition of Rack.

The construction of the rack illustrated by Fig. 104, p. 96, will require the following canes: Four for the legs, each a little over 20 in. long (to allow for bending); four 18-in. canes to form the borders of the sides; a piece to form the handle; and the

canes to complete the rack, the lengths of which can easily be obtained from the illustrations.

Another design for a music rack is given in Fig. 105, and, compared with Fig. 104, the principal differences are that it has three compartments, has

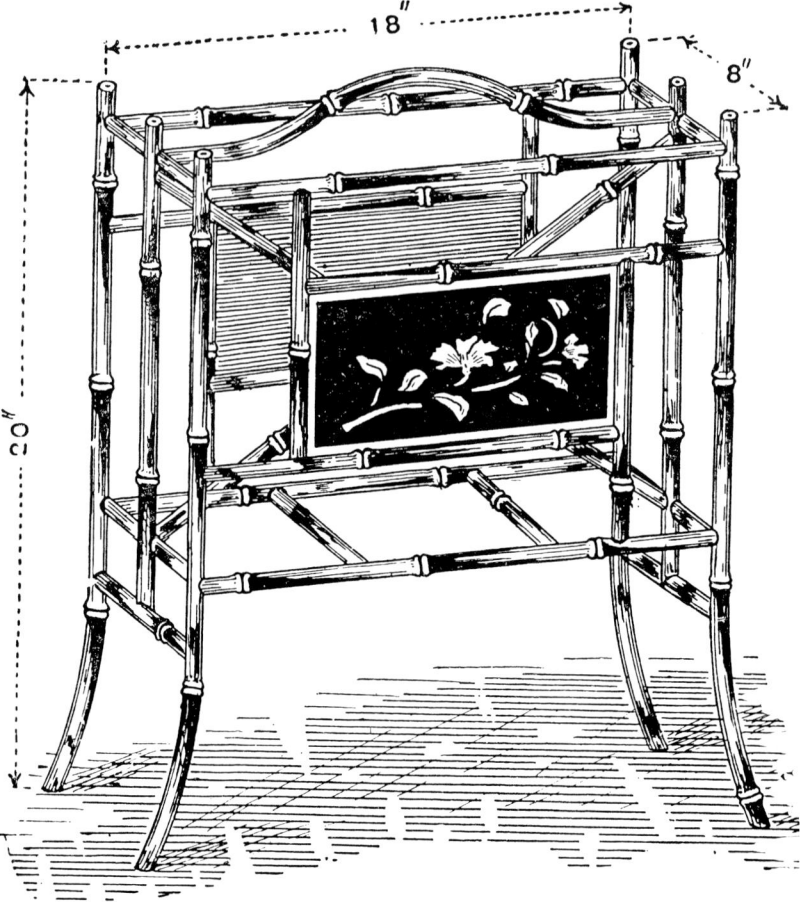

Fig. 104.—Two-Division Music Rack.

handles at the ends, and is provided with casters. The ends of the rods to which the casters are fixed must be plugged with a piece of wood about $1\frac{1}{2}$ in. long. The tops of the four corner uprights are 22 in. from the ground; the rack is 20 in. long, and 14 in. wide.

For the panels some Japanese paper will be wanted. First cut two pieces of wood of the required size and about ½ in. thick, after which cover one side of each with the Japanese paper—thin glue being used for fixing. When this is dry, secure the panels

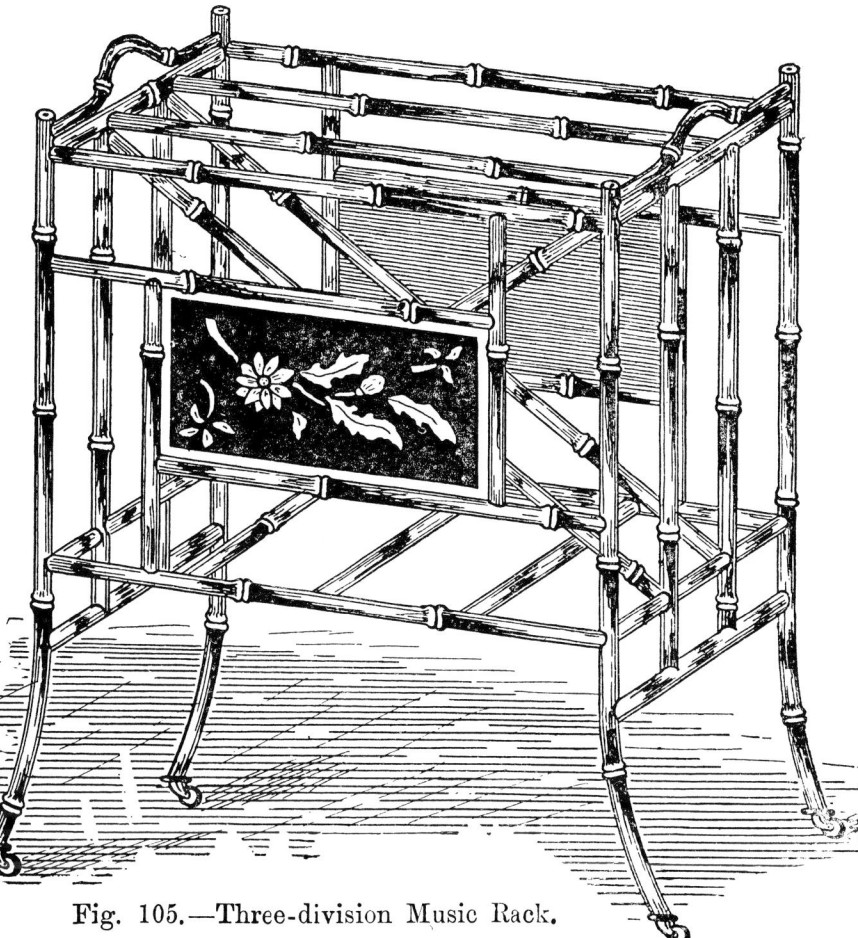

Fig. 105.—Three-division Music Rack.

to the sides of the rack by means of strips of split beading cane. Pieces of millboard are fastened to the backs of the panels.

Fig. 106, p. 98, illustrates a combined table and music canterbury, made in brown bamboo canes about 1 in. thick. It may be about 28 in. high and

G

12 in. deep, and is made in flat sections, A, B, C, D. Fig. 107 shows the construction of sections B and C. Make up the top, put in the panel, hollow out the tops of A and D (Fig. 106), and fix dowels, so that the top of the table will fix on to the dowel. Let the dowel project ½ in., so that the end will fit on to the under side of the top, in the corners of which four holes should be bored to receive the dowels. Hollow out five lengths for rails, to make up 10½ in. long. When all the sections are thoroughly dry—

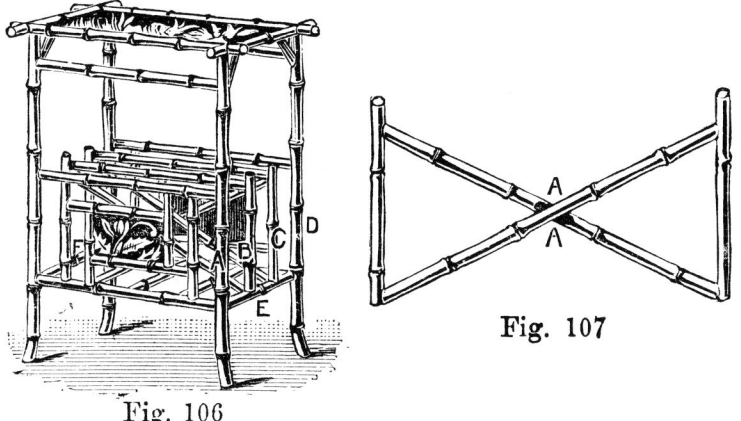

Fig. 106

Fig. 107

Fig. 106.—Combined Table and Music Rack. Fig. 107.— Section of Music Rack.

say in twenty-four hours — take two rails, and bore holes 3 in. from each end to receive dowels ; take sections B and C (Fig. 106), the bottoms of which should be rasped to fit on to the stretchers, and dowelled. Fix the three centre rails to D, and when B and C are set, fasten the whole together. It is advisable to dowel the rails E and F into A and D, as they bear the greatest part of the weight of the music. Fix the top, clamp up, and screw together.

CHAPTER VIII.

BAMBOO CABINETS AND BOOKCASES.

THE bamboo cabinet illustrated by Fig. 108 on the next page is about 6 ft. 8 in. high, and for its construction 18 canes $1\frac{1}{4}$ in. in diameter, and 6 lengths $\frac{1}{2}$ in. to $\frac{3}{4}$ in. in diameter will be required, the lengths being as imported—about $6\frac{1}{2}$ ft.

The back frame (Fig. 109, p. 101) is made first. The uprights A A are 6 ft. high, and must be perfectly straight. The horizontal rails B are mortised at each end, and are made from $1\frac{1}{4}$-in. canes. Bore holes in the uprights with a $\frac{5}{8}$-in. centre-bit, 2 in., 38 in., and 67 in. respectively, from the top of the upright. Then plug the rails with dowels not less than 8 in. long, shave the ends to fit in the holes in the uprights, and fit the frame together. The front frame (Fig. 110, p. 102) is made in the same manner, the uprights being canes 36 in. long, slightly bent at the bottom. Plug them at the top and bore holes at 1 in. and 31 in. from the top to receive the two long rails. Then fit in the rails C, Fig. 109, as follows:—First cut four canes of the $1\frac{1}{4}$-in. bamboo about 34 in. long, and mortise one end. Let this rest on one of the rails between which it will fit and then mark where it touches the other; mortise to the mark, plug, and secure with 3-in. pins. Fit the small horizontal rails in the same manner.

The small slanting pieces shown in Fig. 108, p. 100, known as "herring bone," are cut from $\frac{1}{2}$-in. bamboo, and are about 4 in. long. They are secured with glue and fine nails. The frame for the Japanese lacquer panel D (Fig. 109) should next be put in. This is made of $\frac{3}{4}$-in. bamboo, the panel being 8 in. wide by 6 in. high.

Fit the rails, shown in Fig. 110, p. 102, to the front frame. For the side rails, six pieces of $1\frac{1}{4}$-in. bamboo, mortised to 18 in. long, are required. Four of these

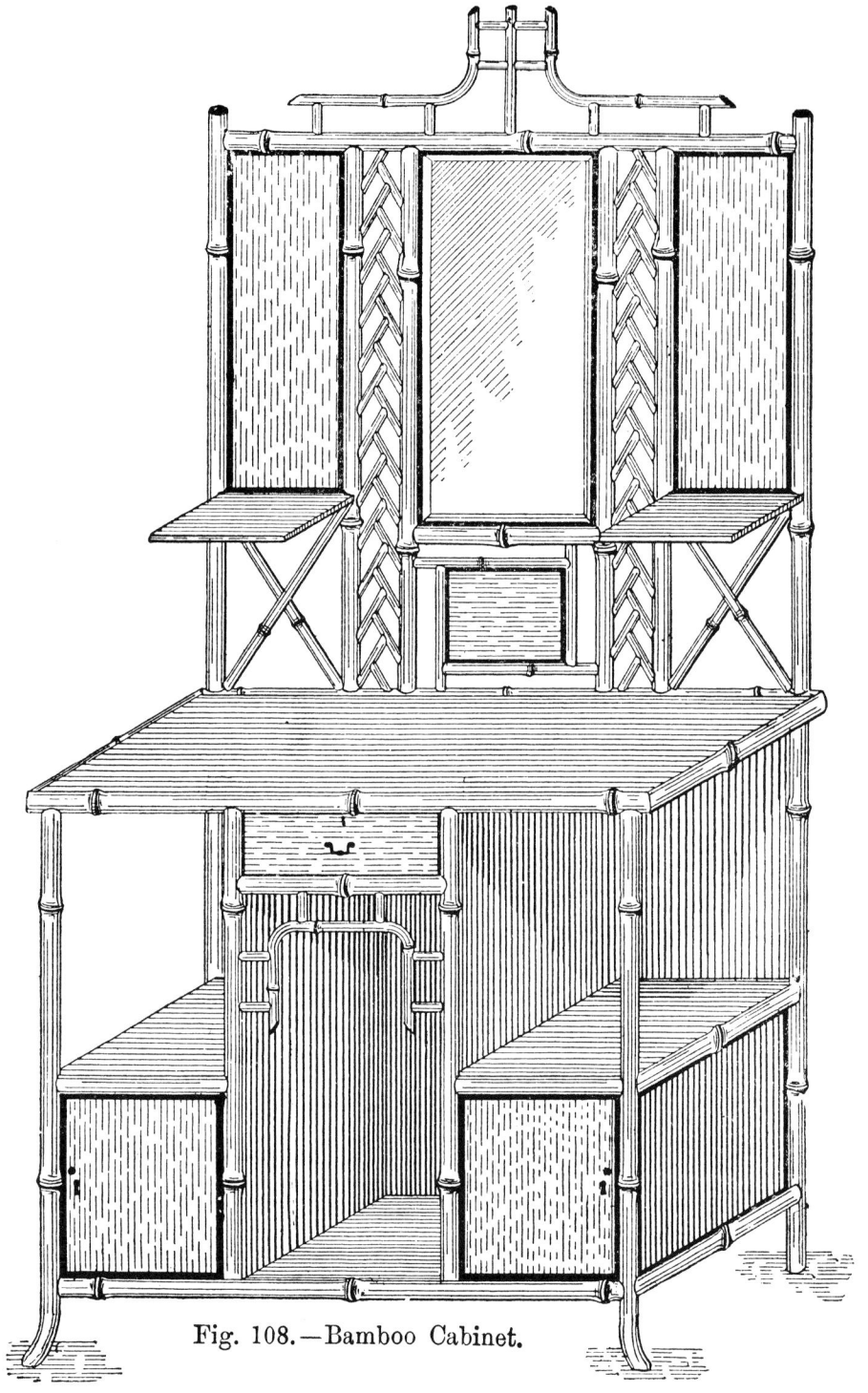

Fig. 108.—Bamboo Cabinet.

go at right angles with the two bottom rails in the back and front frames, the other two being dowelled on 12 in. from the bottom rail. The curved pieces seen in Fig. 108 are of ½-in. stuff. The centre piece in the top rail is 10 in. high, and the curved pieces are spindled to this with pieces of cane 4 in. long.

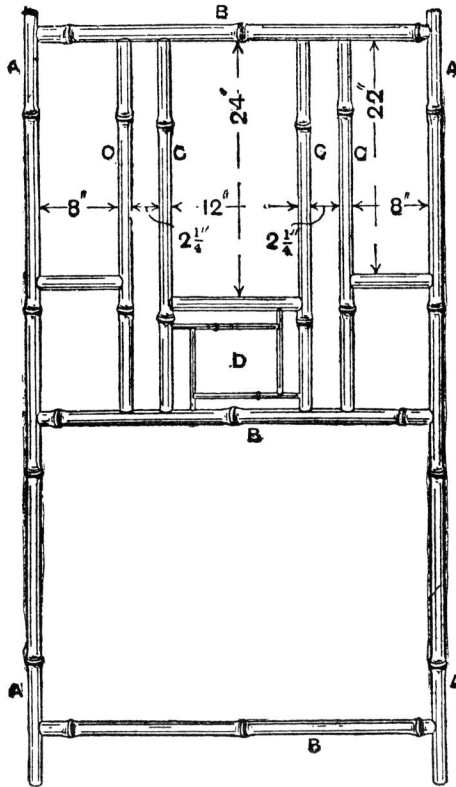

Fig. 109.—Back Section of Bamboo Cabinet.

For the woodwork of the lower part of the cabinet, ½-in. pine is used. Commence by fitting the panels at the back with 2½-in. panel pins, which enter through the bamboo rails. Plane up on the outside, and cover the inner side with Japanese paper. The other parts are done in the same way. The sideboard top is of deal, and projects 3 in. at the sides and the front, split bamboo being fixed on the edges as shown. This is screwed to the uprights in the back frame, and to the plugs in the top of the front uprights. The sideboard top can be covered with Japanese paper, or, if preferred, it could be stained and polished.

The cupboard doors are made of Japanese lacquer with split bamboo nailed round the edges, and are fixed with brass hinges. A small lock or a brass cupboard turn fastens the door. The drawer is of deal, a piece of Japanese lacquer forming the front panel, a brass handle being screwed on as shown. The glass in the top part of the cabinet is of 24-in.

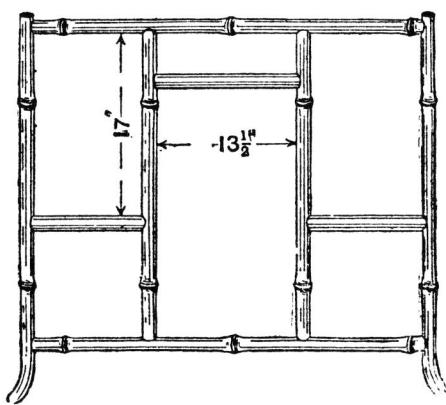

Fig. 110.—Front Section of Bamboo Cabinet.

by 12-in. bevelled edge plate, and is fixed in a rebate formed by a split cane nailed to the bamboo. A wood panel is fixed at the back. The large panels at the sides of the glass are of Japanese lacquer, as are also the two shelves, the latter being fixed with screws driven from the back of the rails, against which they rest. The cabinet, with the exception of the panels, which are polished when imported, should have a coat or two of white shellac varnish (see p. 39).

Fig. 111 shows a cabinet bearing some general resemblance to the previous one. The uprights of top are 2 ft. 6 in. long, the cross rails 3 ft. 3 in., and the mirror 20 in. by 15 in.   Use 1¼-in. or 1½-in. canes for the work.   Make up the front and back of the cabinet in the first place, and, while these are setting, get out the back of the top.   Join together the two bottom sections.   The distance between front

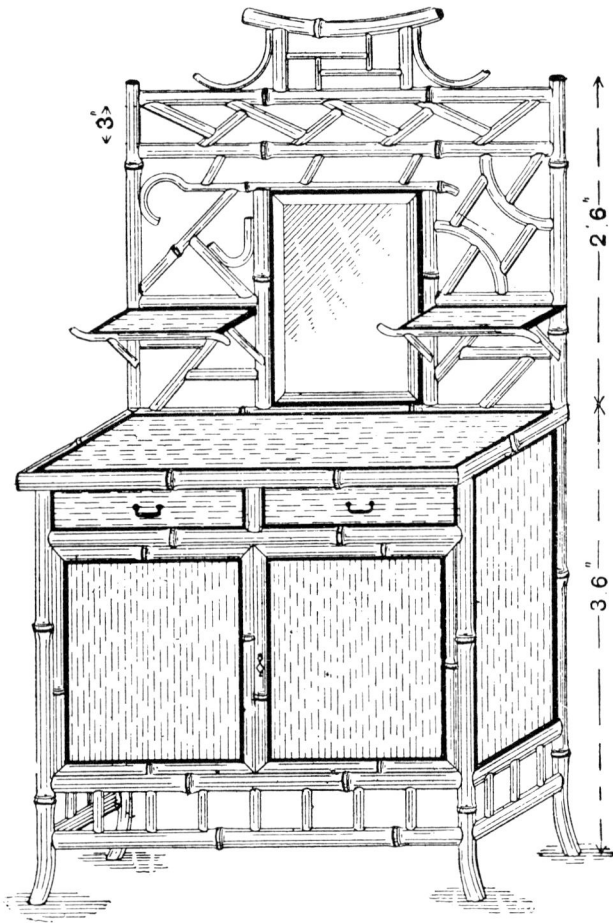

Fig. 111.—Bamboo Cabinet.

and back rails is about 10 in. if the cabinet is to be 13 in. deep over all.   Make the door frames from perfectly straight 1-in. canes.   These canes should be mitred at the corner, and a right-angle dowel should be used for filling.   The rebate for the glass

should be formed with split black cane.   The doors are hinged on pins, which act as pivots.   The construction of the upper portion of the work is very similar to that described for the making of an over-mantel illustrated by Figs. 152 and 154, pp. 135 and 138.

The bamboo music cabinet illustrated by Fig. 112 is first framed up in two sections, A and B (Fig. 113). The two front legs should not be cut off to length until they have been bent, and 2 in. should be al-

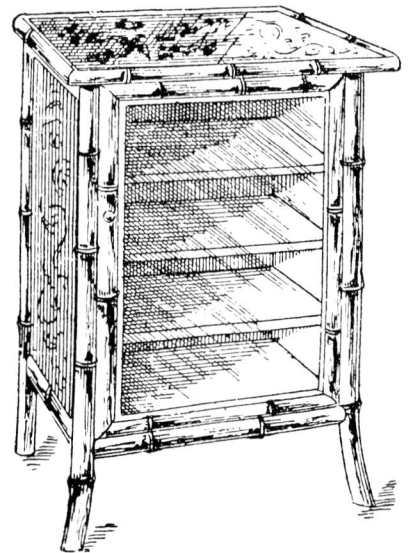

Fig. 112.—Bamboo Music Cabinet.

lowed on the rails for chisel-pointing and fitting. Care must be taken to get the sections perfectly square.   They should be thoroughly tested with the measuring lath.   While the sections are setting, the four side rails C (Fig. 113) should be fitted, and the whole frame afterwards put together.   The back, sides, and bottom of the cabinet are made of ½-in. deal, covered with Japanese leather paper or matting.   The sides are fixed in position with nails, driven through the four legs, but before this is done any knots in the bamboo should be rasped down, so that the wood may fit close in the frame. The shelves can next be fitted, after which the sides are beaded with split cane, white or black. The mottled or tortoised appearance on some of the beading is produced by passing the cane through a flame and burning it at intervals (see p. 38).

The door frame, in Figs. 112 and 114, is shown made from whole cane, which should be slightly smaller than that used for the legs. Great care must be taken to use canes both straight and of

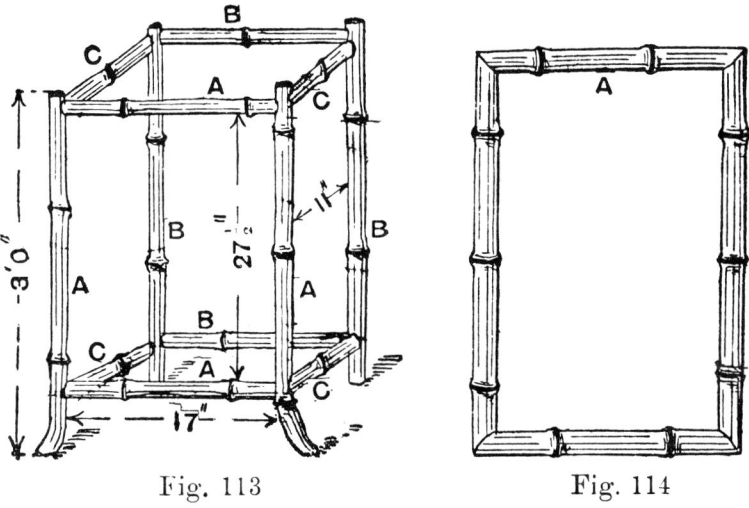

Fig. 113

Fig. 114

Fig. 113.—Framing of Bamboo Music Cabinet. Fig. 114. —Door Frame of Bamboo Music Cabinet.

uniform thickness. First rasp down all protruding knots, and then cut off the four pieces in a mitre box ; fit them in the places they will occupy inside the frame A, Fig. 113. After being marked, they are taken out and a rather long dowel is fitted into the end of each, one end of the dowel being allowed to project. When all the ends are fitted, the frame should be laid down flat, with each piece in its proper position, and the two dowels on A (Fig. 114) taken out, mitred, and nailed together. Each angle should be treated in a similar manner, and the whole frame then tem-

porarily fitted together and tried in its place. If it fits correctly it can be glued up and left to set. A fine nail is put through each mitre to strengthen the joint further. All knots on the door frame should be rasped down flat, and a rebate formed with split beading cane to receive the glass. The door, hinged on pins, is fastened by a cupboard turn, which should be made of sheet brass so that it can be bent to the shape of the bamboo. The four rails should now be cut off close to the top cross rails, and the whole top surface levelled up to receive the top. This is made from a good lacquer panel, 20 in. by 14 in., beaded with whole bamboo. For whole beading a very straight cane should be chosen, and one side planed flat. The beading should be mitred and fixed in place with 2-in. panel pins driven through the bamboo into the lacquer. As has been said again and again, do not drive a nail through bamboo without first boring a hole for it, otherwise the cane will split. The mitred corners should be just touched with glue, and the squareness of the corners taken off with a rasp. An inside beading of black cane greatly improves the appearance of the top. A covering of $\frac{1}{2}$-in. wood, the size of the lacquer panel, should be screwed to the top of the cabinet frame, and the lacquer top screwed to it from underneath, care being taken that the screws do not go through the lacquer.

A combined china cupboard and bookcase in bamboo is illustrated by Fig. 115 ; it is made in two sections, the bottom one, which serves as the cupboard, being made first. From $1\frac{1}{4}$-in. or $1\frac{1}{2}$-in. canes cut off four pieces each 38 in. long for the legs, and four pieces each 36 in., which will be $33\frac{1}{2}$ in. after being rasped and fitted. Now fit and make up the two sections marked A and B (Fig. 116, p. 108), and set aside to dry. While the sections are setting, the rails C to form the frame should be got out and fitted, and when the two sections are dry the whole should be fitted together and the tops of the legs sawn off straight and plugged. The wood to fill in the sides and back of the frame should now be got out. The inside of the cupboard may be either stained and varnished, or covered with Japanese leather paper; the outside

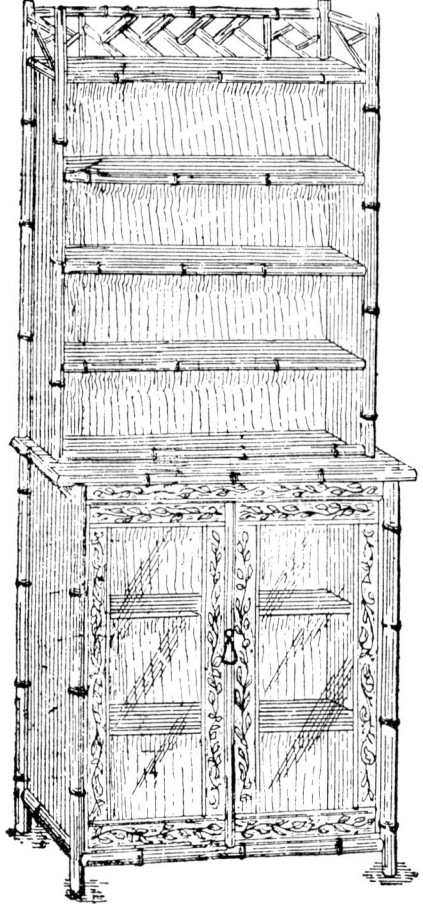

Fig. 115.—Combined China Cupboard and Bookcase.

may be covered with leather paper or matting, according to taste. The shelves should be fitted into their places (see pp. 110 to 112) and then the frames of the two doors prepared. These are made from deal 2 in. wide and $\frac{5}{8}$ in. or $\frac{3}{4}$ in. thick. They are illustrated as being covered with leather paper

and slipped with split cane. The inside slipping of cane is made to project and so to form a rebate for holding the glass in position. Unless some true-sawn cane as prepared for dado work is at hand, it is advisable to run the plane along the split bamboo in order that it may fit perfectly level on the wood. The doors are hung on pins. A nail should be driven into the bottom of the door frame, and allowed to project about $\frac{1}{2}$ in., and a hole made in the bottom of the frame to receive it. The top pin is passed

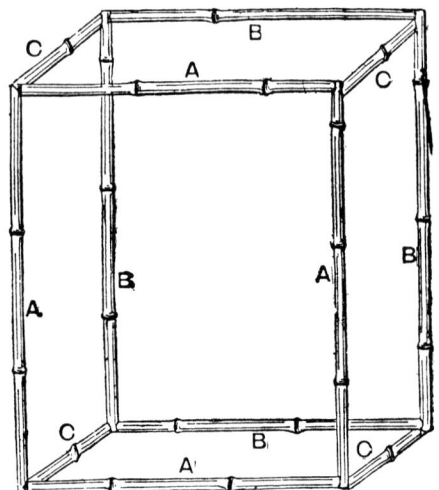

Fig. 116.—Framing of China Cupboard.

through a hole bored in the top rail into the top of the door frame. The doors are fastened with a small bolt and cupboard turn. The top of the cupboard is made from $\frac{3}{4}$-in. stuff, and should be 39 in. long and 14 in. wide, so that it overlaps $1\frac{1}{2}$ in. at each side and 1 in. at the front. It should be screwed on to the frame and afterwards covered with leather paper, matting, or lacquer panels. If the latter are used, they should be fastened to the wood with fine nails round the edge, so that the nails will afterwards be covered with the inside slip of cane when the edge has been slipped with split bamboo.

The making of the upper section—the bookcase proper—will now be described. From 1¼-in. or 1½-in. canes cut off four pieces each 3 ft. 6 in. long to form the uprights, and five pieces each 35½ in. long (2 in. being allowed for fitting) to form the rails of the sections A and B (Fig. 117). These should be put together as before described, care being taken to get the whole work firm and square. The rails C (Fig. 117) should be got out 10 in. long (2 in. being allowed for fitting), and when the sections are dry the whole should be framed together. It must now be decided whether the shelves are to be fixtures or

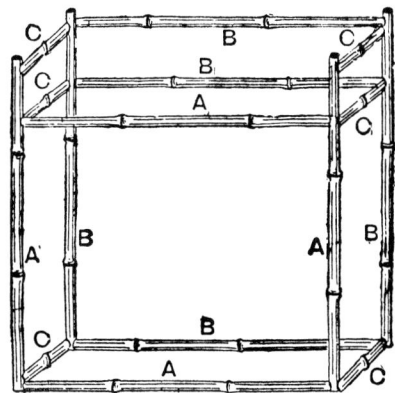

Fig. 117.—Framing of Bookcase.

movable. Having decided upon the kind of shelves to be employed, the sides and back of the bookcase should be fixed in position, care being taken not to make too close a fit or the joints will be sprung. The filling at the top is next done. The herringbone work in the centre is started from the left-hand side, and is put in piece by piece, each piece being fastened with glue and fine beading pins. The shelves for the bookcase should have a slipping of split cane the exact thickness of the shelf, and a leather shelf-edging should be fastened on underneath to make a good finish.

Bamboo bookcases are much firmer if they have a wooden back as in Fig. 115; there is difficulty sometimes in supporting and securing the shelves of bamboo bookcases, but the following plan answers well:—Insert a screw-eye at the requisite height for each shelf in each bamboo upright, diagonally. Notch the shelves slightly at the corners to fit the bamboo uprights; lay them on the screw-eyes, and

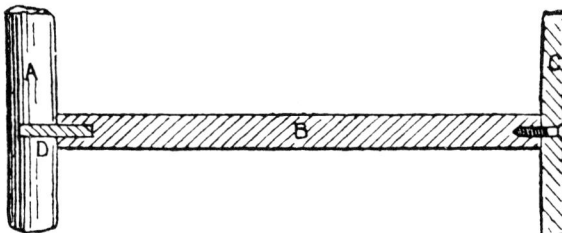

Fig. 118.—Method of Fixing Bookshelf.

through each eye, from the underside, insert a screw, which will hold all rigid. The fixing of the shelves all depends on the kind of bookcase; if, as in Fig. 115, p. 107, the back is of wood, the following method of fixing them might be adopted: Screw or dowel through one of the front bamboos at each end of shelf, so as to fix it, and to keep the shelf from sink-

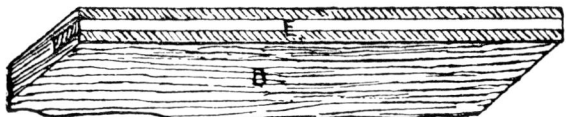

Fig. 119.—Bookshelf Grooved and Tongued.

ing in the middle widthways. Plough a groove across each end, and insert a hardwood tongue as shown in Figs. 118 and 119. In Fig. 118, which is a section, A is the bamboo; B, shelf; C, back; and D, dowel. Fig. 119 shows end of shelf, with tongue inserted; B indicating the shelf and E the tongue.

Bookcase shelves may rest directly on the rails, the upper surface of the latter having the nodes rasped off, so that the shelf can fit level. In such a case the shelf should have a very slight projection over the rail, and its edge should be moulded or chamfered, and cut out at the angles to take the upright bars (see Fig. 120). After being fitted properly, small screws, driven up from the underside of the rails, will secure the shelf. Another way is to fix the shelves flush with the upper surface of the rail. The inner face should be rasped off level, and a small section taken out of the cane to receive the

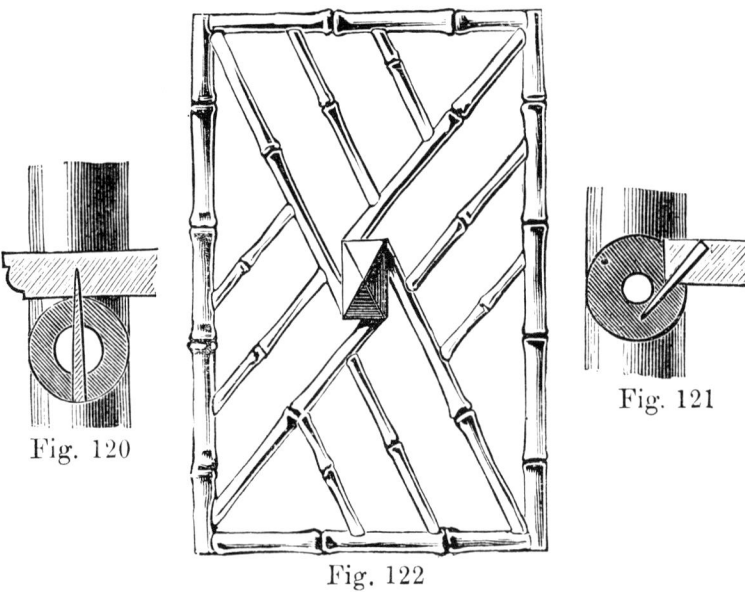

Fig. 120   Fig. 121

Fig. 122

Figs. 120 and 121.—Methods of Supporting Bookshelves. Fig. 122.—Bamboo Side of Bookcase.

shelf as in Fig. 121. The shelf might be further secured by driving in small screws through it into the rail.

For the wooden sides of bamboo bookcases, may be substituted ornamental work formed of small canes, something like Fig. 122; this is more in keeping with the framework than are boarded sides.

The bamboo bookshelf shown by Fig. 123 is suitable for standing on a writing-desk in a recess 5 ft. wide. Four strong mottled bamboos are cut

to 5-ft. lengths, and these, without any further work upon them, form the horizontals shown by Fig. 123. Four uprights, 19 in. long are required, and, in cutting them, leave one of the natural joints of the wood as a finish for the top. These uprights are framed together with shorter pieces, as shown by Fig. 124, the joints being formed by plugging the ends of the short pieces and drilling holes in the uprights. The plugs are glued into the cross-pieces, and a wire nail is driven into the uprights afterwards to make all secure. The 5-ft. lengths are then laid on these

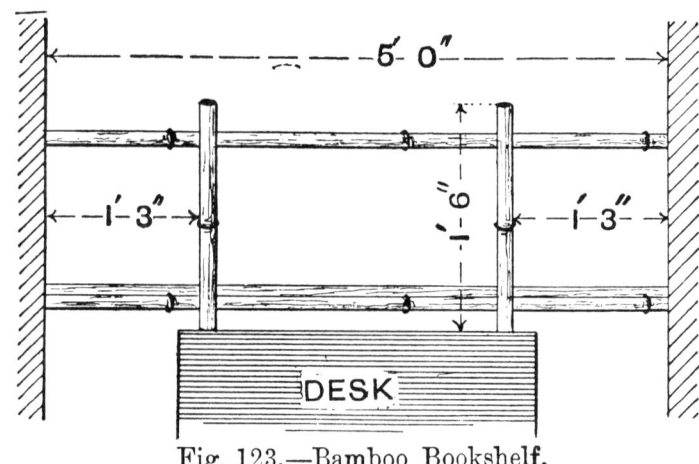

Fig. 123.—Bamboo Bookshelf.

frames and a nail put through each one to secure it to the frames. As the whole thing is made to fit comfortably into a recess, diagonal bracing is not required, the walls preventing anything getting out of place. Otherwise it will be necessary to provide braces in the direction in which additional strength is required. The shelves are planed up from $\frac{3}{4}$-in. cypress or other wood, stained walnut, and varnished. The bottom shelf rests on the two bamboos. The top shelf is made narrower and drops between the two upper bamboos, as it is not intended to take any heavy weight. Neatness is gained by concealing its front edge behind the horizontal bamboo.

Fig. 125 shows an upright writing-stand in bamboo, about 3 ft. high, 2 ft. wide, and 9 in. deep, with a top slightly overlapping. The writing flap should be 15 in. deep, and can either be hung with ordinary hinges or pivots. The stand can be of rough wood, as it is covered both inside and out either with Japanese paper or matting—the former for preference—and further relieved by panelling the sides

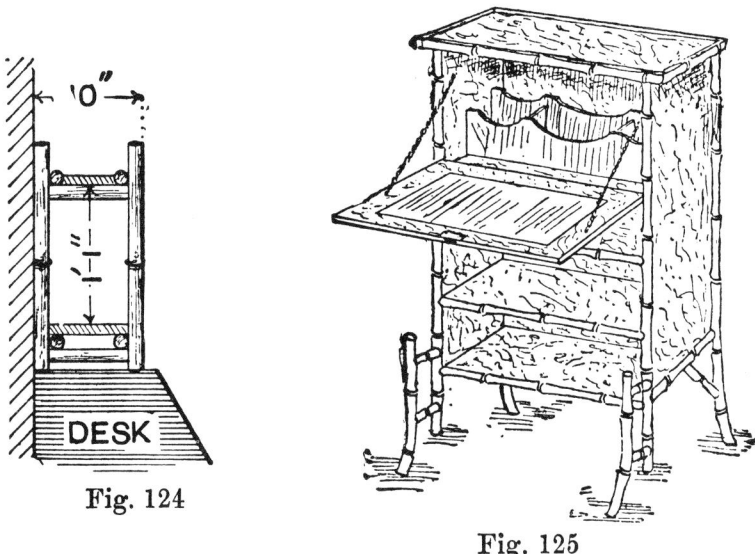

Fig. 124

Fig. 125

Fig. 124.—End View of Bamboo Bookshelf. Fig. 125.— Bamboo Writing-stand.

with split bamboo. By pivoting the flap is meant that it swings on two stout wire pins fixed through the front bamboo; but it can also be hinged in the ordinary way with brass hinges to the shelf. The four uprights should be of whole bamboo, but the front of shelves and other parts need only be of split bamboo, which is really preferable, as it does not stand out too prominently. The flap is supported by brass chains, and should be covered inside with leather or leatherette. A design for another writing-table is given on p. 54.

CHAPTER IX.

BAMBOO WINDOW BLINDS.

BAMBOO window blinds have several advantages over cane or lattice blinds; they do not discolour, they are easily cleaned and dusted, and when old their appearance can be brightened by a coat of clear spirit varnish. No dimensions for the blinds described in this chapter are given, as each must be made to suit the window it is to occupy. In measuring for the blind, the exact distances between the beads of the window frame must be taken, and these will form the outside measurements for the width of the blind. For the blind shown by Fig. 126, two or three lengths of 1-in. bamboo and about half a dozen lengths of $\frac{1}{2}$-in. bamboo will be required. From the 1-in. bamboo cut off two lengths to form the uprights A (Fig. 127) and two lengths to form the cross rails B. A suitable length for the uprights would be from 18 in. to 21 in. long. For the hollowing of the ends the cross rails should be cut 2 in. longer than required, this amount being left for the thickness of the uprights A. The ends of the cross rails to be hollowed should first be chisel-pointed with a saw and then finished with a bamboo rasp. One end of each cross rail must be fitted first, after it is pointed, and hollowed with a $\frac{1}{2}$-in. round rasp to as nearly as possible the size of the cane. Owing to the irregularities of bamboo, each joint must be fitted separately. The rails and uprights should be marked to prevent any mistake in gluing up. One end of each cross rail should be fitted to its respective upright, and the other end marked; this will give the bottom of the hollow. Then it can be fitted in the same manner as the first. In putting together the other ends, take care that the hollows fall in the same plane as the first, otherwise they will not fit together when the two uprights are parallel to one another.

Next join the four pieces into a section. The cross rails are dowelled to the uprights, the dowels

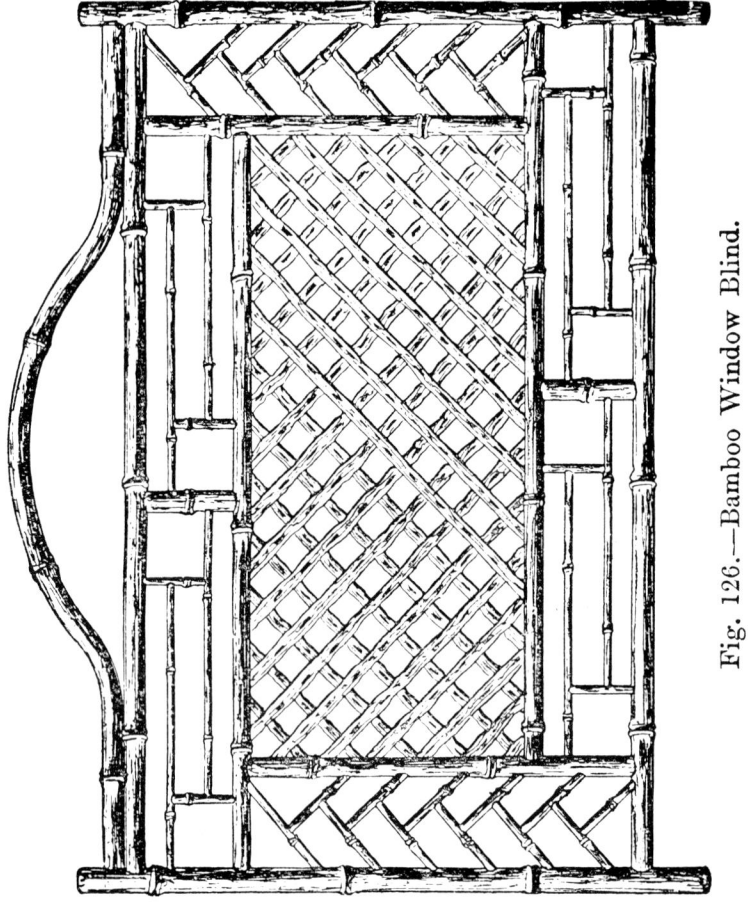

Fig. 126.—Bamboo Window Blind.

end in the manner illustrated by Fig. 127 and described on pp. 232 and 24. When the section is square, it should be placed on one side until the glue sets.

In the centre of Fig. 126 a Japanese lattice-wood panel is shown. As these panels can be obtained

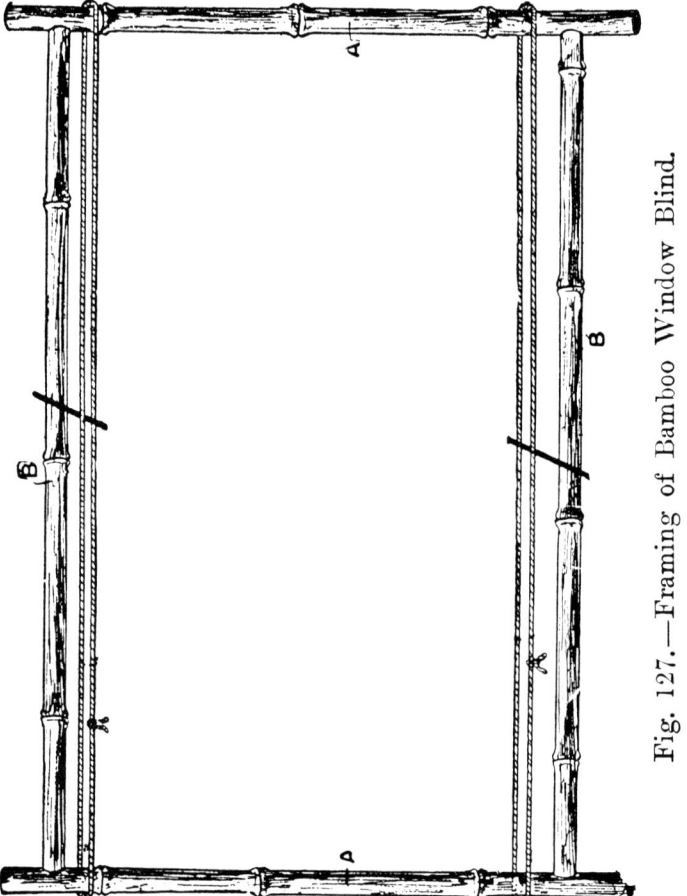

Fig. 127.—Framing of Bamboo Window Blind.

being fitted first to the cross rails and then to the holes in the uprights. The two cross rails must be attached to one of the uprights first, the second upright being added afterwards in the same way, the gluing being done as quickly as possible. When the frame is together it must be clamped at each

only in the following sizes, the inside section must be made accordingly. The sizes are : 9 in. by 9 in., 12 in. by 9 in., 12 in. by 12 in., 12 in. by 15 in., and 12 in. by 18 in. While the section is setting, make the inner frame for the lattice-wood panel. Cut four pieces from the thick ends of the ½-in. canes to form the frame (Fig. 128). The lengths should be chisel-pointed and dowelled at one end. The space for the panel should be measured, the holes for the dowels bored, and the sections fitted and glued together. The small oblong fillings outside the panel can now be made, and the whole allowed to set. When the large section is set, it should be placed in the position it is to occupy in the outer frame, and marked. Dowels should be fitted and then fixed by boring a hole through the outer frame with a bradawl and fastening with a panel pin. The four small sections

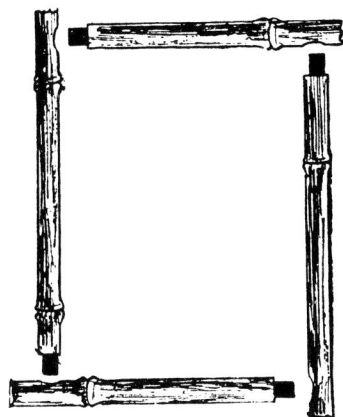

Fig. 128.—Framing for Inside Section of Blind.

then can be fitted and fixed with glue and ¾-in. beading pins. To fit the lattice work, commence at the top, each piece being fitted and held in position with glue and beading pins as the work proceeds. The top of the screen will require bending to shape.

The construction of the blind illustrated by Fig. 129, p. 118, is similar to that just described. The fan can be made in two pieces, and the ribs should be made from small bamboo. The pediment, or top of this screen, can be glued into holes bored in the top of the cross rail.

The window blind illustrated by Fig. 130, p. 119, should not present difficulty in making. The filling at

the sides is commenced by forming the cross and then adding each piece as in the lattice work. To fix the leaded light, first rasp down any knots on the inside of the frame, and make a rebate of split rattan cane, carefully mitred at the corners and fastened

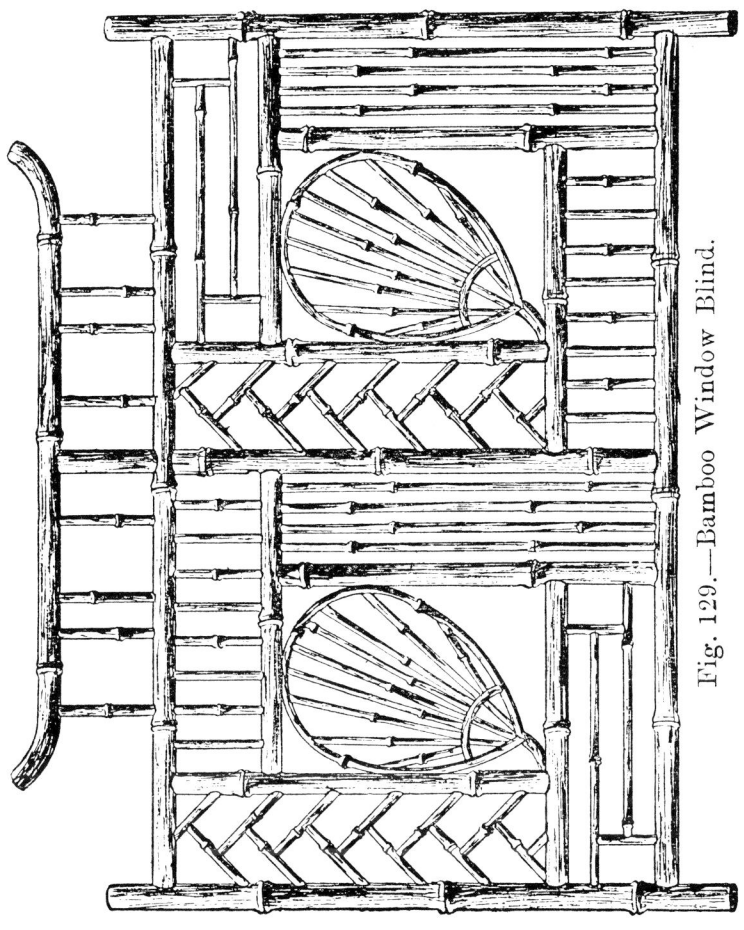

Fig. 129.—Bamboo Window Blind.

on with beading pins, for a support. The glass should then be placed in position and fastened on the other side in the same manner. The whole of the work should have a coat of spirit varnish when finished.

Either of the bamboo window frames shown by

Figs. 131 and 133, pp. 120 and 121, is an artistic addition to any room. That shown by Fig. 131 is for a window that is flush with the wall, the top and sides of the frame on this account standing out for a distance of about 9 in. One of these sides is shown by small cane, the latter being used for the twists and bends. Two lengths of $\frac{7}{8}$-in. tortoiseshell bamboo, bent at each end and fixed to the two front poles about 6 in. apart, form the top, and a design is built up between these in a similar manner to that adopted

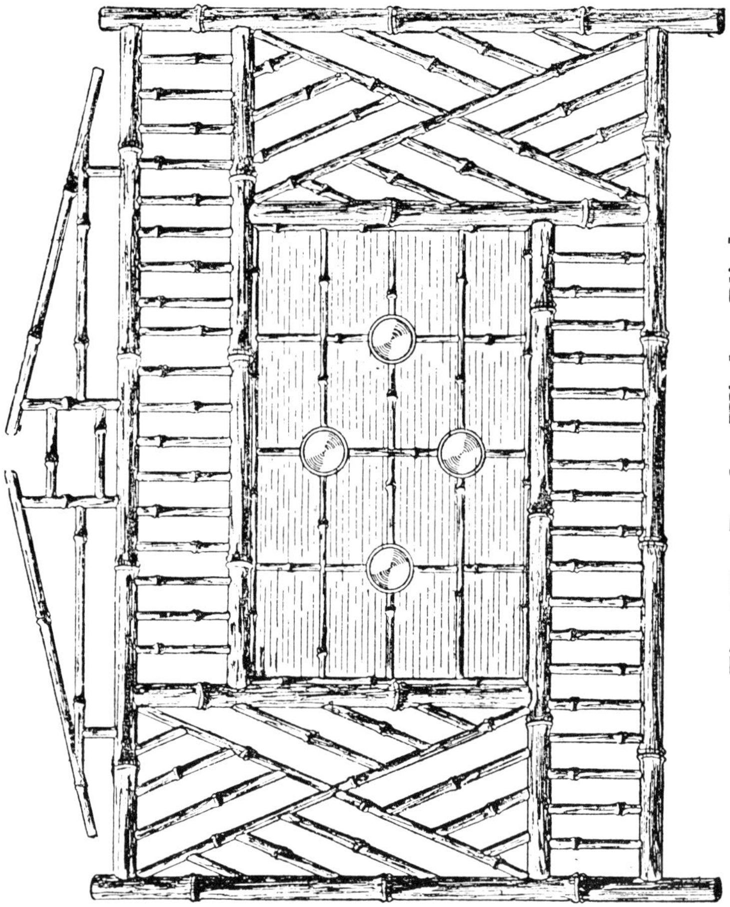

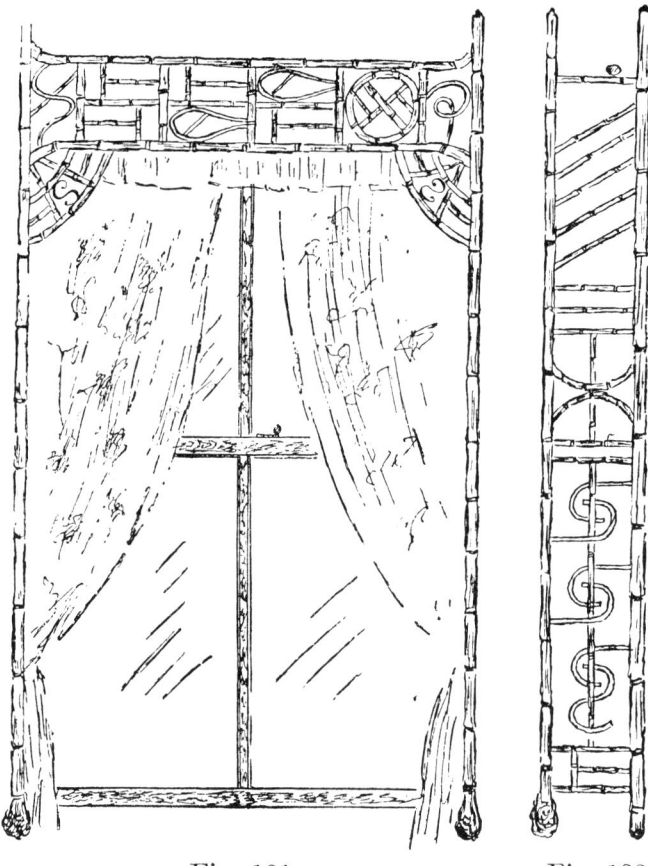

Fig. 130.—Bamboo Window Blind.

Fig. 131   Fig. 132

Fig. 131.—Bamboo Frame for Window Flush with Wall.
Fig. 132.—Side View of Bamboo Window Frame.

Fig. 132. The two front tortoiseshell canes are each about 6 ft. long, and may have root ends at the bottom, although this is not essential. The two back canes which rest against the wall are $1\frac{1}{4}$ in. in diameter and are of the same lengths as the front two, and between these the sides are built up in any desired design of $\frac{1}{2}$-in. tortoiseshell bamboo and for the sides. The two fancy corner angles are of $\frac{1}{2}$-in. tortoiseshell bamboo bent and fitted, and are fixed to the top and sides. The curtain is suspended by means of the usual hooks and eyes to a bamboo pole which rests upon the two uppermost cross-bars on each side of the frame.

The frame shown by Fig. 133 is for a recessed window, and is simply a frame with sides and top about 9 in. wide fitting flat against the wall around the opening of the window; it is made similar to the one described above, ¾-in. tortoiseshell bamboo,

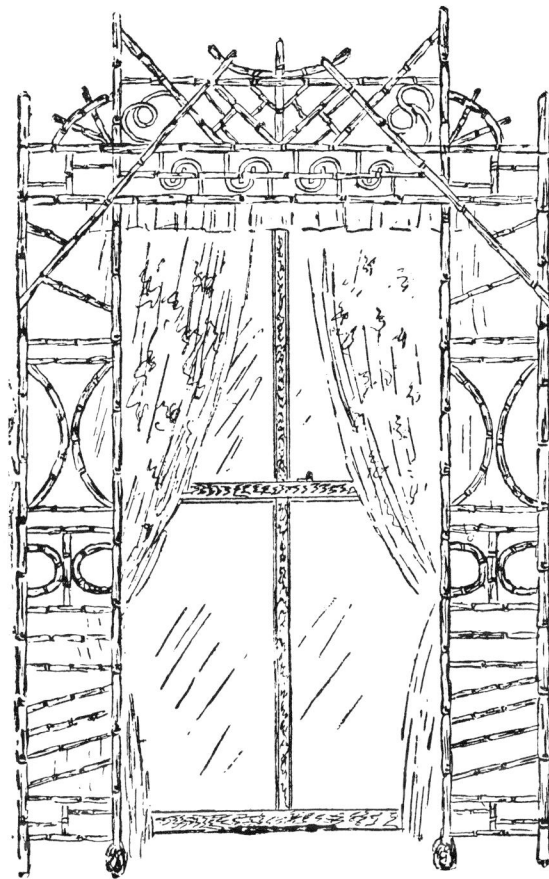

Fig. 133.—Bamboo Frame for Recessed Window.

however, being used for the slanting pieces at the top. The curtain in this case is supported by the pole running across the frame at the top. When everything is finished a good coat of varnish should be given to the whole, and the frame fixed to the wall by means of staples or other suitable fastening.

CHAPTER X.

MISCELLANEOUS ARTICLES OF BAMBOO.

IN this chapter will be illustrated and described a variety of bamboo articles, chiefly household furniture, that are now coming into popular use.

The coal-box shown by Fig. 134 is of novel design, practical in its construction, and forms, when closed, a comfortable settee. It consists of a wooden box and hinged lid, covered with fancy matting or Japanese embossed paper, and surmounted with an edging of bamboo dado or split bamboo. The box is mounted on four crossed legs of bent bamboo, and within the box is the usual loose iron lining. The lid is hinged with brass strap hinges, and on the side is a brass strap to hold the hand-scoop. The box can be made of any rough wood, and measures inside 18 in. long, 13 in. wide, and 9 in. high; the bottom, lid, and sides need be of ½-in. wood only, and the end pieces ¾ in. thick. The width necessitates a glued joint in the lid. Get a yard of matting —which is a sufficient quantity to cover the box on the outside and the lid on the two sides—and cut it to size. Have plenty of good, hot thin glue and apply it liberally to both the wood and the matting, particularly if the wood has a rough surface, when naturally it will absorb more; apply pressure until the glue has set, otherwise the matting will only stick in places and look lumpy. The same applies equally to Japanese paper; and, as regards the matting, it is better to cut it rather fuller than the size actually required, and when glued trim off any surplus with a sharp knife (see also p. 51).

The cross-legs are practically the only troublesome parts of the coal-box; to make them, get four

1-in. bamboo canes with root ends, which should be trimmed up first by burning them well in a gas jet or with a spirit lamp and rasping them close down, but not to destroy the appearance of the root. The

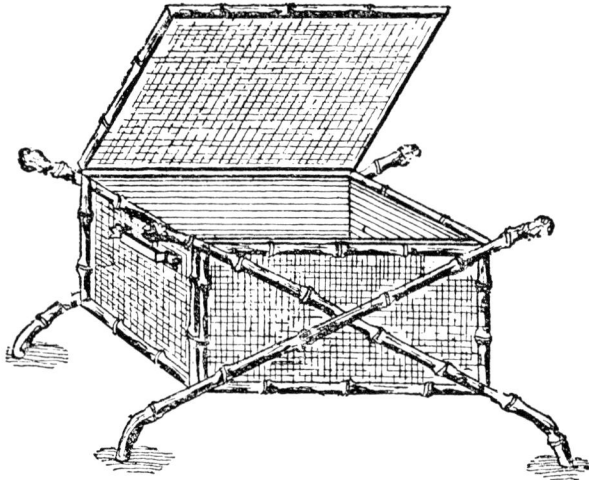

Fig. 134.—Bamboo Coal-box.

bamboos as imported are 6 ft. 6 in. long; and for the legs do not cut any off until they are bent to the required shape, for the greater the leverage the better the bend.

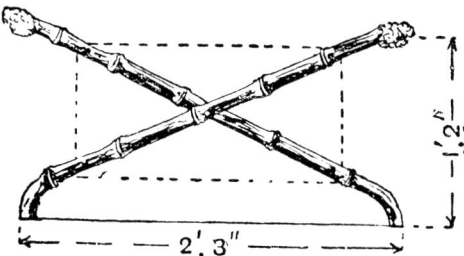

Fig. 135.—Legs of Bamboo Coal-box.

If space will admit of it, chalk out the shape of a leg on the floor, and taking $9\frac{1}{2}$ in. as the height of the box outside, plan it out as shown in Fig. 135, the box when mounted being 4 in. from the floor,

and the bottom and top ends of each leg extending about the same distance on either side; then, by bending each leg to correspond with the chalked plan, they are sure to be exact. If, however, space is limited, place the box on its side and bend one leg to the required shape, trying it several times during the process of bending, and, taking the first one as a pattern, bend the others to it.

Having cut off the legs to their proper length and plugged the foot end, proceed to fix them to the box, laying the box on its side and fixing one with two 2-in. round-headed brass screws into the ends of the box, taking care to drill all holes for screws first in the bamboo, or it will split. Then take the

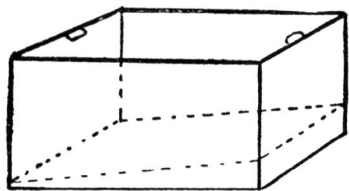

Fig. 136.—Iron Lining for Bamboo Coal-box.

second leg, lay it across in its proper position, and mark the under one with a pencil where the top one crosses; then they are halved out, and having thus fitted one into the other, screw on the second leg, and also put a screw through where the two legs cross; then turn the box over and proceed with the other side.

The bamboo dado is formed by splitting canes in halves lengthways; the canes can be bought ready split. The width for the sides and ends is $\frac{3}{4}$ in., and $\frac{1}{2}$ in. for the lid; and in the case of the latter it is fixed on to the edges. The dado or edging for the ends of the box can be fixed before the legs are screwed on, the corners being mitred, but the edging on the sides is put on after the legs are fixed. The bamboo for the lid being fixed on the edges, a strip of black or white split beading cane is fixed on the top side as a finish off ; and it is better to hinge the lid on first before putting on the dado, and be careful to see it does not interfere with the lid closing flat.

The hinges are those known as brass strap coal-box hinges ; they are made in a fancy pattern, and screwed on the outside with round-headed brass screws. The lining which holds the coals should be made of No. 24 B.W.G. sheet iron with folding handles for lifting out and is best made in galvanised iron ; if made in black iron it should be well japanned to prevent rust ; it is illustrated by Fig. 136,

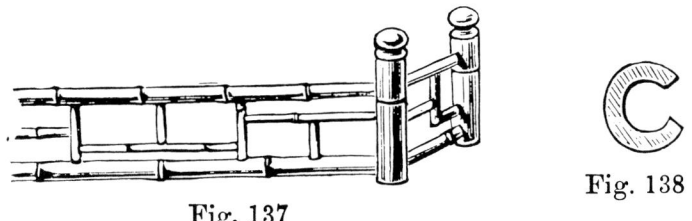

Fig. 137

Fig. 137.—Bamboo Fender. Fig. 138.—Section of Cane with Strip removed.

which also gives a sectional view of the bottom ; this, it will be seen, is made on the slope, thus enabling the coals to be easily got at.

A fender (Fig. 137) is easily made ; take two stout bamboos long enough to make the sides and front. Where the bend is to be, rasp out two holes as shown, and bend them round the uprights. The ends and centre-bars can be let in holes bored with a brace and bit. The bottom, or tray, should be made of sheet brass, cut to fit, and fixed on the ends of the uprights (which should be plugged and pinned) with stout screws.

Fern-cases and aquaria can be made partly with bamboo, the framework being formed of canes that have each had a strip about a third of their circumference cut out by a cutting gauge (Fig. 11, p. 25).

Fig. 138, p. 125, is a section of a cane so treated. Saw out notches to allow of angle joints being made (see Fig. 139), and fit in the glass with red lead. The cross-pieces lap over the angles where the bamboos are glued together. Scrape off the natural polish with a piece of glass or roughen with a rasp to provide a better holding surface for the glue. Use the square freely ; make all joints true, and bind them together with stout twine, which should not be

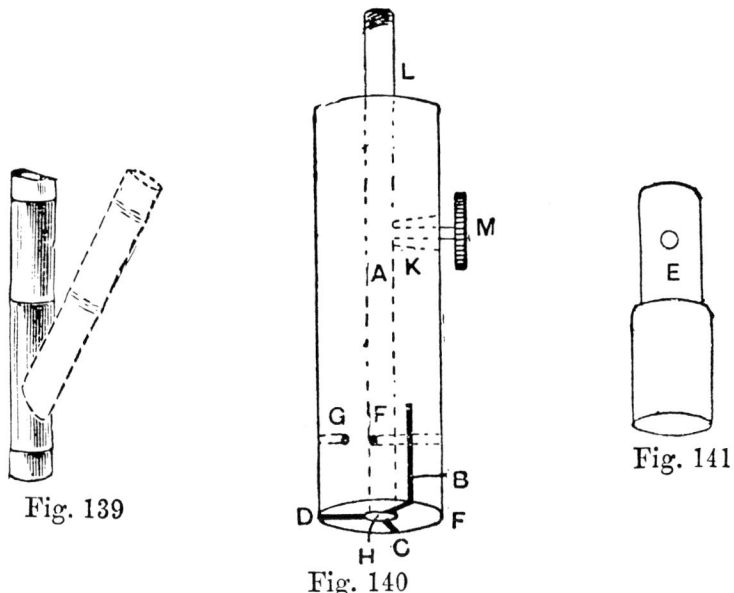

Fig. 139

Fig. 140

Fig. 141

Fig. 139.—Angle Joint for Aquarium. Figs. 140 and 141. —Bamboo Camera Stand.

removed for two or three days if possible, although this is not absolutely necessary. The work may, when done, be French polished.

Picture-fames can be made of bamboo if a section is cut out as shown in Fig. 138, p. 125. The mitres can be made as described on p. 34, and illustrated by Fig. 24. It will be necessary to plug the ends of the canes. A bamboo photograph frame is illustrated on p. 141.

A small bamboo stand for supporting a light

camera may be made as follows :—Prepare a cylindrical block of hard wood as A (Fig. 140), boring it through the centre and making cuts B, C, and D. Into these fit firmly the flat hinge blades E of the caps (Fig. 141), passing a pin or rivet through each on which the caps turn (see dotted lines F and G). Through the central hole H pass a brass rod L about

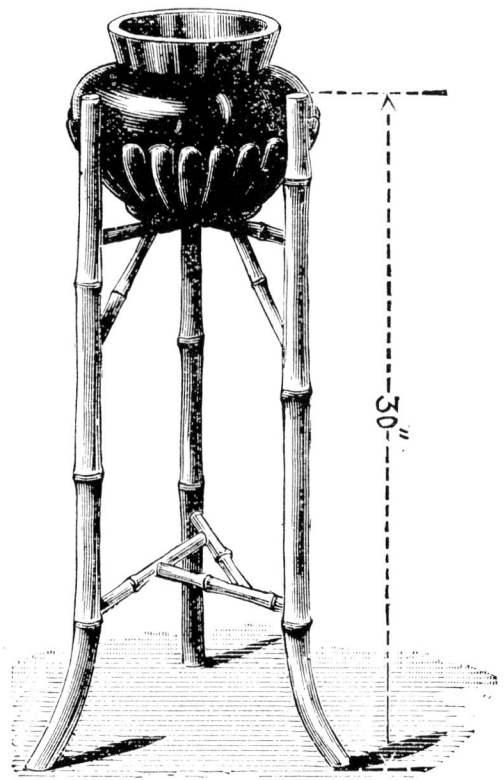

Fig. 142.—Flower-pot or Jardinière Stand.

1 ft. long with a screw thread cut on it, to go into the camera base. At K insert a coarse-thread nut to take a thumb-screw M, which bites against L, for fixing it at any height. Fit each of three small bamboo canes with ferrules and insert tightly in the metal caps, and the stand is complete.

For the flower-pot or jardiniere stand shown in Fig. 142, select three canes about $\frac{3}{4}$ in. diameter for

the uprights, and curve them at one end to form the feet. Curve them before cutting to precise length. The cane first bent should be used as a guide for the other two, in order that the three may be curved alike. From $\frac{1}{2}$-in. cane cut off six lengths, each 10 in. ; fit, dowel, and clamp up as shown in Fig. 143. With a brace and small bit bore holes in the uprights

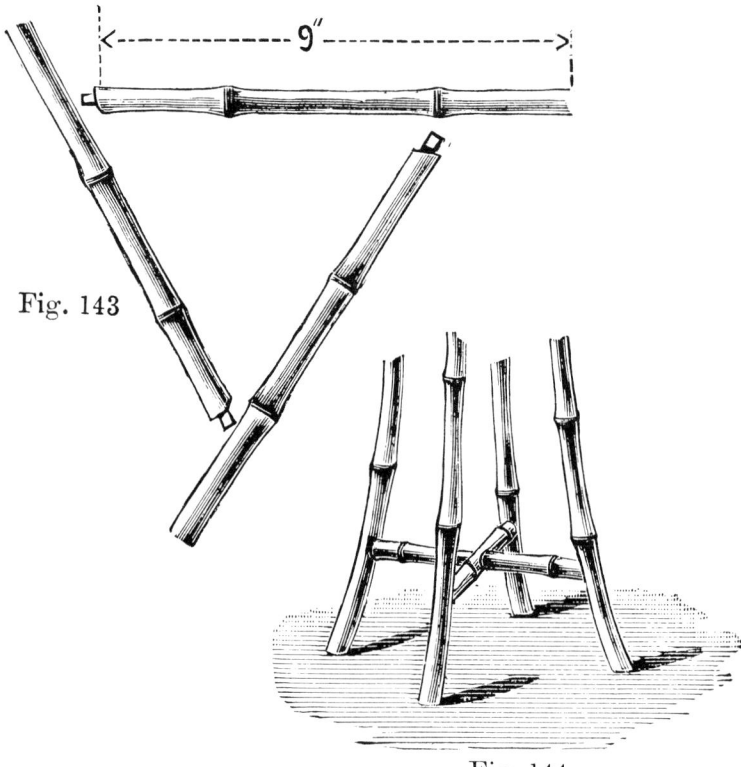

Fig. 143.—Triangle for Bamboo Stand. Fig. 144.—Alternate Design for Flower-pot Stand.

to receive the triangles, about six inches from the bottom and top. Fix the triangles (first having plugged up the outside ends) in the bored holes in the uprights ; glue, and fasten with a 2-in. wire nail. As shown in Fig. 142, three 5-in. stays are fastened at the top ; these pieces are dowelled, rasped to fit, and fixed in their places with fine wire nails.

The bottom portion of an alternative design is shown by Fig. 144, in which are four uprights connected together by a cross, which consists of one cane with a dowel through the centre, and two pieces fitted to the dowel on either side (see Fig. 30, p. 36). Fig. 145 shows the top of a tripod to support a flower-pot or jardiniere; the construction of the bottom may be the same as in Fig. 142. The tops

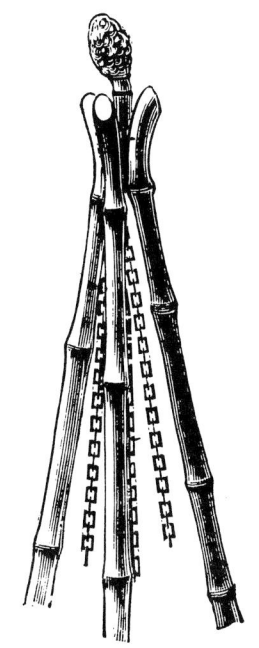

Fig. 145.—Bamboo Tripod for Jardiniere.

are slightly bent out, and a rasped root fastened in the centre. This is plugged at the bottom and a hook inserted for the hanging pot.

Fig. 146, p. 130, is a view of a bamboo flower-stand which will hold three pots. For the centre, which should be 3 ft. 3 in. high, use $1\frac{1}{4}$-in. cane, and for the three supports, 1-in. cane. The three spindles should be of $\frac{3}{4}$-in. cane, 14 in. long, plugged at each end, and let into the centre cane at one end and into supports at the other. The supports are

screwed to the centre cane with $1\frac{3}{4}$-in. round-headed screws. The lengths of the three supports should be made to correspond with the size of the pot to be placed on the shelf. The heart-shaped shelf is of $\frac{3}{4}$-in. deal, covered with matting, and slipped round with split bamboo; or, if preferred, two rows of thick rattan (beading cane) can be used in preference. The shelves are screwed on through the centre rod, and supported by two struts fastened

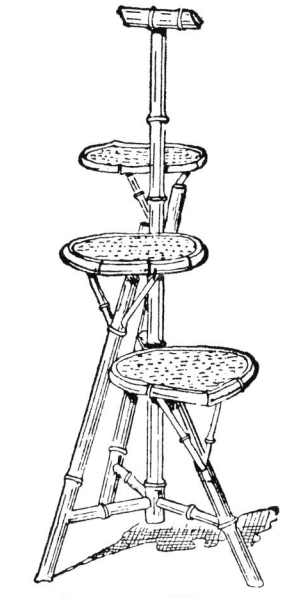

Fig. 146.—Bamboo Flower-pot Stand.

to the supports with 1-in. panel pins. The centre rod is mortised at the top and dowelled, and a piece of $1\frac{1}{4}$-in. bamboo is cut for the handle, which is screwed into the centre-rod.

A bamboo flower-pot stand for the window is shown in side and front view respectively by Figs. 147 and 148. $\frac{3}{4}$-in. canes are used for uprights and horizontal pieces, and where they cross file notches in the uprights, and fasten them together with screws; $\frac{3}{8}$-in. canes are used for the diagonal pieces, and let into the horizontal ones just through one side. The

I

lengths of the necessary canes are : For the two ends, parts A and B (Figs. 147 and 148), four pieces each 22 in. long ; two pieces for c 16 in. long ; two for D 10 in. long ; four uprights, J and K, 3 ft. long ; two for I 2 ft. 6 in. long ; two for H 2 ft. long. These are laid out as shown in Fig. 147, and the position of the holes for the diagonal stays marked and bored. The stays then are put in the holes, and the whole

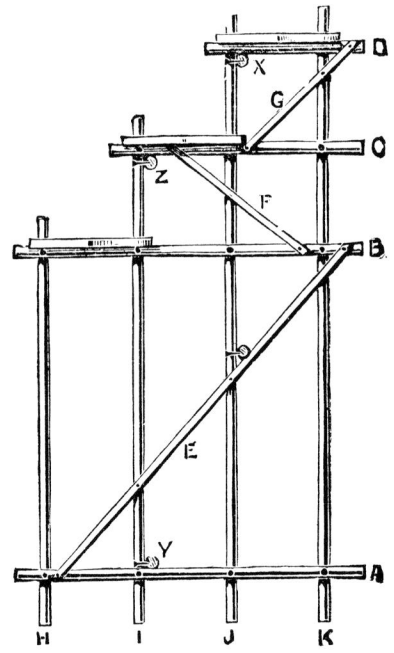

Fig. 147.—Bamboo Flower-pot Stand for Window.

fastened with screws. Having made the two ends, the three shelves are next wanted ; $\frac{1}{2}$-in. stuff $7\frac{1}{2}$ in. wide may be used, and the holes in them must be a good fit for the cane ; the top shelf can then be put on, but the other shelves must have pieces cut out of the side, as shown in Fig. 149. When the shelves are on, the stand will be fairly firm, but to make it more so, stays are put from w and w', to x and x', and from Y to z, Fig. 148 ; these pass the back of the shelves, and are screwed to them.

As has frequently been remarked in the foregoing pages, bamboo canes lend themselves to the construction of all articles of furniture that, necessarily strong, are preferably light and graceful also. More especially is this fact to be noted in the case of flower-pot stands and lampstands, which have to support heavy weights and so must be strong and serviceable ; the collapse of either article would be particularly annoying, and in the case of the lamp-

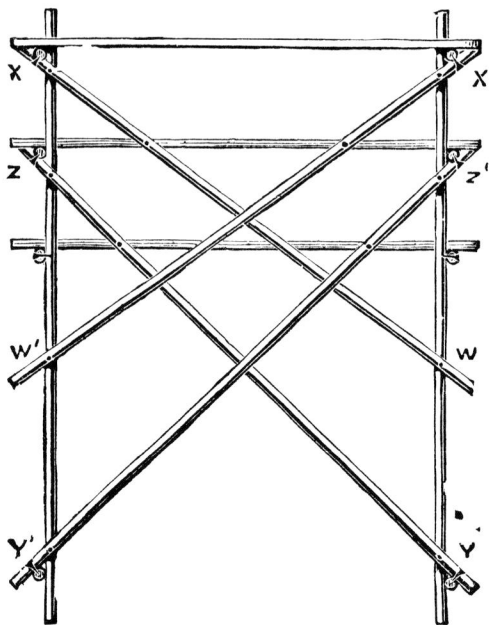

Fig. 148.—Bamboo Flower-pot Stand for Window.

stand, would be attended with much danger, were the lamp in use. All bamboo lamp-stands should be carefully weighted (see p. 44) to prevent top-heaviness. It may be remarked that many stands serve equally well as either lamp or flower-pot supports.

A very simple tripod lamp-stand is shown by Fig. 150. To prevent the stand upsetting, break through the knot at the bottom of each stick, fill it with sand, and plug the end ; also fix a piece of sheet-lead underneath the shelf. Tripod lamp-stands are usually about 5 ft. high, the ring to hold the lamp being fixed about 4 in. from the top. This ring is 8 in. or 9 in. diameter, made of stout

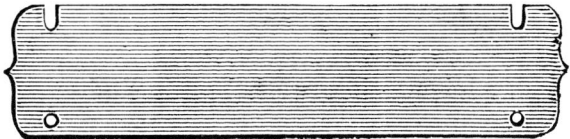

Fig. 149.—Shelf of Window-stand.

beading cane spliced together. The legs at the bottom should be at least 18 in. apart, the shelf being triangular with equal sides, made up of wood covered

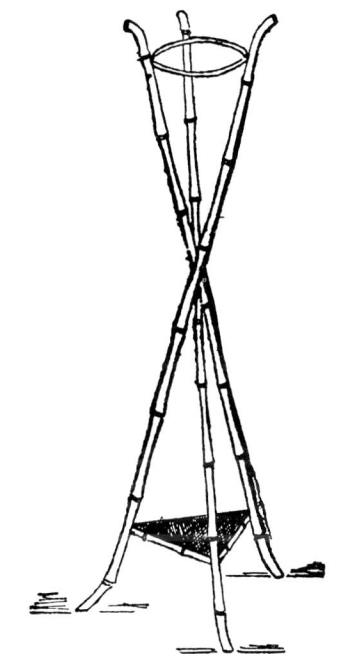

Fig. 150.—Bamboo Lamp-stand.

with matting or Japanese paper and edged with bamboo. The bottom ends of uprights are slightly bent outwards to give the stand a firmer holding, the uprights being of 1¼-in. bamboo.

For the lamp-stand (Fig. 151) take three long, stout bamboos. Three-legged articles always stand firm—that is, they do not rock as a four-legged table does sometimes, especially where the floor is not quite level; and where a lamp is concerned this is a very important consideration. Bend the legs and tops to hold the reservoir of the lamp. Bind the standards together with bands of brass, copper,

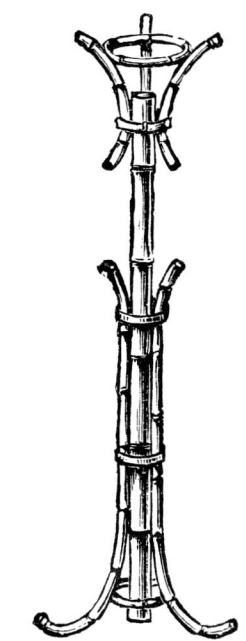

Fig. 151.—Bamboo Lamp-stand.

or wrought iron; or they may be glued and pinned only. Beauty and strength are added to the work by using ornamental copper bands, pierced with trefoils, quatrefoils, or, if possible, ornamented by repoussé work. The top, to hold the oil container, should be made of a band of metal, although it is quite possible to make it of bamboos, bent in a circular shape and joined together by wooden plugs pinned and glued in. It is, however, rather difficult to bend bamboo into a perfect circle. Whether the ring is of bamboo or metal, it is fixed with screws.

One way of making a bamboo overmantel is first to construct a frame of wood, which should be rebated to hold the glass, especially if this is to be heavy plate. The front surface could then be

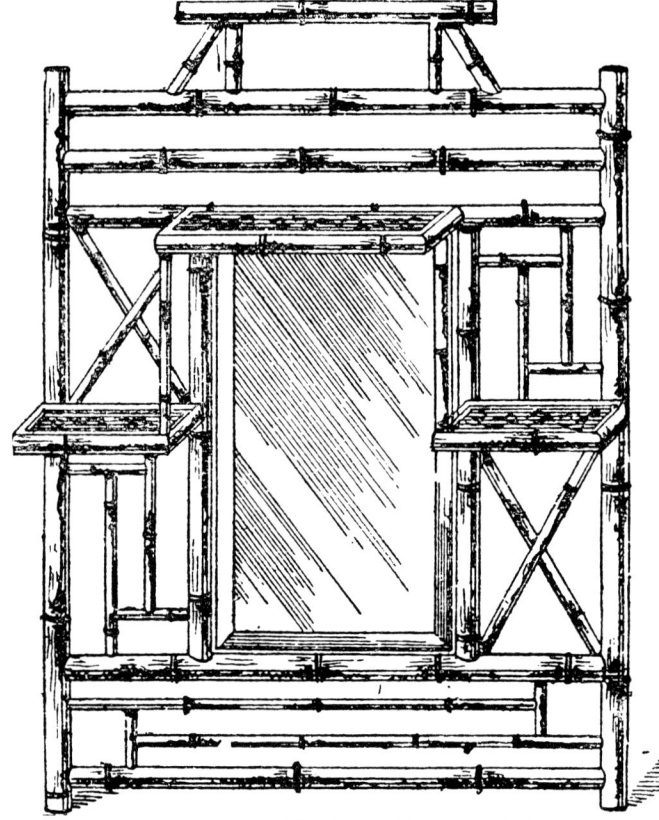

Fig. 152.—Bamboo Overmantel.

covered over with split bamboos, fixed on with very fine French nails or screws and a little glue. Another way is to cut a small strip out of the cane lengthways (Fig. 138, p. 125), and fit together with mitre-joints. In this method the glass must be fitted in before the last side is fixed on, and there is also a danger of the canes warping or twisting and breaking the glass,

especially if it be at all thin. Probably the easiest way is to build up the foundation of plain deal, which can afterwards be painted brown, and covered all over with bamboo as described above. Whether the joints should be simply halved or mortised depends upon the quality of work required.

A simple bamboo overmantel is illustrated by Fig. 152, p. 135, and Fig. 153 shows the back of it. The canes used should be $1\frac{1}{4}$-in. for the uprights and rails, and $\frac{5}{8}$-in. for the filling. Cut off two pieces, each 36 in. long, for the uprights, and five pieces, each 30 in. long, for the rails. Fit the rails on to the uprights, remembering that the irregular character of bamboo does not allow of the substitution one for another of parallel parts such as these rails. The uprights should be bored and fitted with dowels, and the whole section framed together and left to dry. While it is drying the filling can be made. The shelves can also be prepared; these should be made either of lacquer, or of wood stained and varnished, or covered with Japanese leather paper. The large shelf should be 13 in. long and 4 in. wide, and the two smaller shelves 8 in. long and 4 in. wide. The front and side edges of these shelves may be slipped with split bamboo nailed on with fine wire nails. When the section is thoroughly set, the two uprights, which are to form the sides for the mirror, should be fitted into their places. The canes should be dowelled, care being taken when gluing in the dowels that they do not project in the least beyond the hollowed edge of the tube; also that the hollowed edge be not injured during the fitting of the dowel. These uprights should be fixed into their places by boring a hole through the cross-rails and fastening with a 2-in. fine wire nail. Care should be taken that the space between these rails is 12 in. wide to allow of the width of the glass; also that the distance between the two cross-rails is 20 in.

Two rails must now be fitted between the outside

and inside uprights, midway between the rails which form the top and bottom of the glass frame, to form support to which the shelves will have to be fixed. The two fillings or "cracks," as they are called amongst bamboo workers, should now be fixed into their places. The cross (X) filling is very simply made; a piece of cane is fitted with the rasp diagonally across the opening to be filled, and fastened into its place with beading pins; two short pieces are now fitted the alternative way, and so the X is

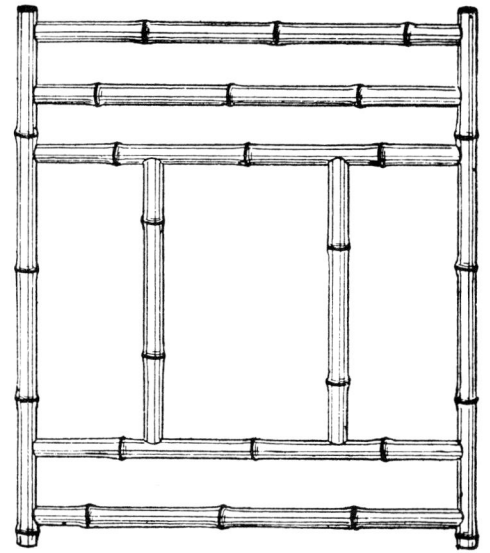

Fig. 153.—Back Section of Bamboo Overmantel.

formed. A piece of bamboo, 14 in. long, for the top of the overmantel, and two pieces, each 4 in. long, to form the uprights, should now be cut. The two uprights should be chisel-pointed, and rasped to fit, the one end on to the top rail of the overmantel, and the other to the rail just prepared. Two holes should be bored in the top rail to receive the end of the wooden dowels, which should go right through the short uprights and lastly be fixed into two holes bored in the top piece at the same distances as in the top rail. The shelves now should be fixed **by** boring

through the back of the rails and fastening by wire nails. Two stays of $\frac{3}{8}$-in. cane should be prepared and fixed into position under the two small brackets; these stays resemble the one shown by Fig. 70, p. 63. A rebate must be formed in the rattan cane for the reception of the glass. Except for cleaning off the surplus glue and varnishing, the overmantel is now finished.

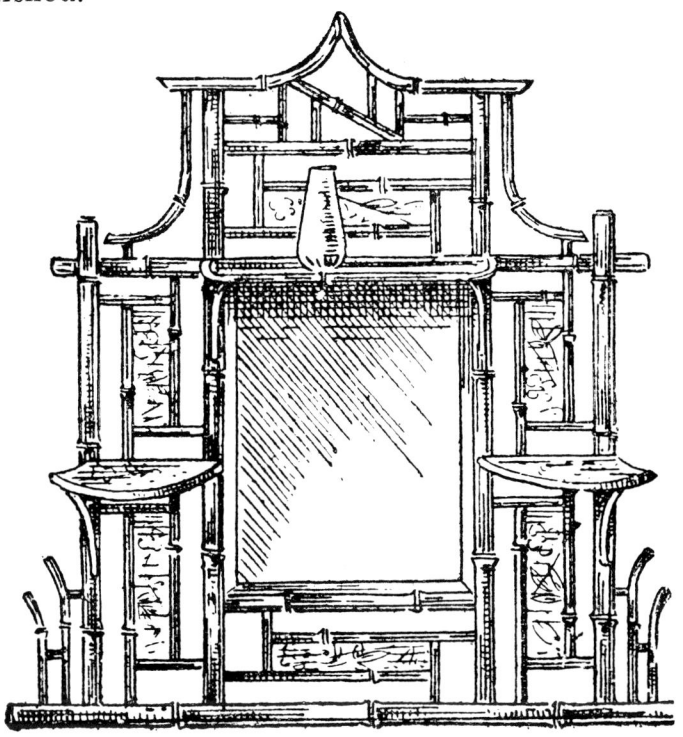

Fig. 154.—Bamboo Overmantel.

Fig. 154 shows a rather more elaborate overmantel, but after the frame (Fig. 155) is squarely made the rest of the work is very simple. From $1\frac{1}{4}$-in. or $1\frac{1}{2}$-in. canes cut off one piece 4 ft. 1 in. long, two pieces each 3 ft. long, and two pieces each 3 ft. 11 in. long, to form the bottom rail and uprights of overmantel. One end of each upright should be chisel-pointed, plugged, and fitted temporarily into the place it will occupy on the bottom rail. The distances are given in Fig. 155. Rails A A, B B, and C should now be got out and fitted (for lengths when fitted, see Fig. 155). To fix the rails B B into position a hole should be drilled through the four uprights the same size as the hollow of the rails to be filled, and a dowel passed through and fastened into the rails at each side. The rails A and C are fitted and

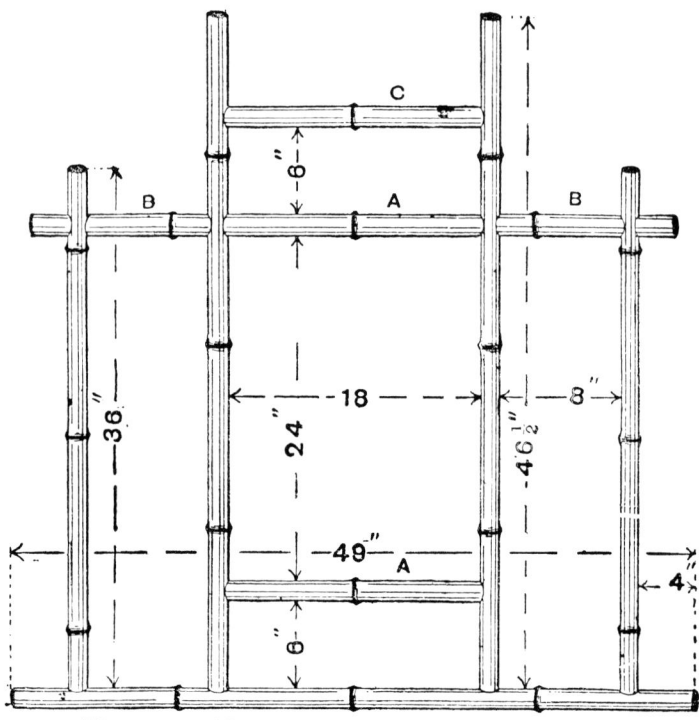

Fig. 155.—Framing of Bamboo Overmantel.

fixed in the manner before described. The centres of the cracks or fillings are made of Japanese lacquer. The easiest size to cut pieces of lacquer is 4 in. wide by 10 in. long, and they must be fastened to the bamboo by wire nails, the angles being hollowed. Then fit the whole together.

A half design of an overmantel is given by Fig. 156, p. 140. Cut four bamboos for the uprights and three for the large cross-pieces, these latter to be

about 2 in. longer than the actual width will be when finished. With a round rasp cut the ends to fit on to the uprights. They can be fastened with glue and a few small brass pins. If required to be extra strong, plug the ends of the cross-pieces with wood, and pin them to the uprights. The shelves

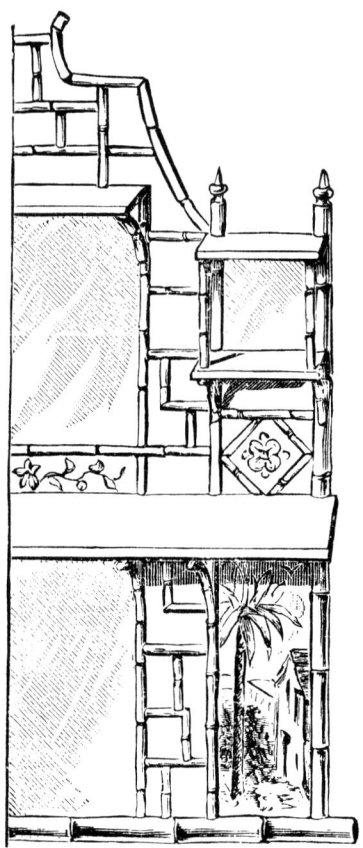

Fig. 156.—Half-elevation of Bamboo Overmantel.

can be made of thin fret-wood, held in position by needle-points or long brads.

A photograph frame is illustrated by Fig. 157. To make it, first obtain some lengths of bamboo of about 1 in. diameter, and cut two pieces, each 17 in. long, for the uprights A (Fig. 157); two pieces, each 17½ in. long, for the outer rails B; two pieces, each 12 in.

long, for the middle divisions C; and three pieces, each 6 in. long, for the small rails D. Plug the ends of the two uprights and shape the ends of the outer rails to fit, cutting them down till there is a distance of 15½ in. between the uprights. Fill up the rails, and nail them to the uprights, leaving a space of 11 in. between them. Place the division rails at equal distances apart, and nail them in, and then put in the small rails so as to leave a space for

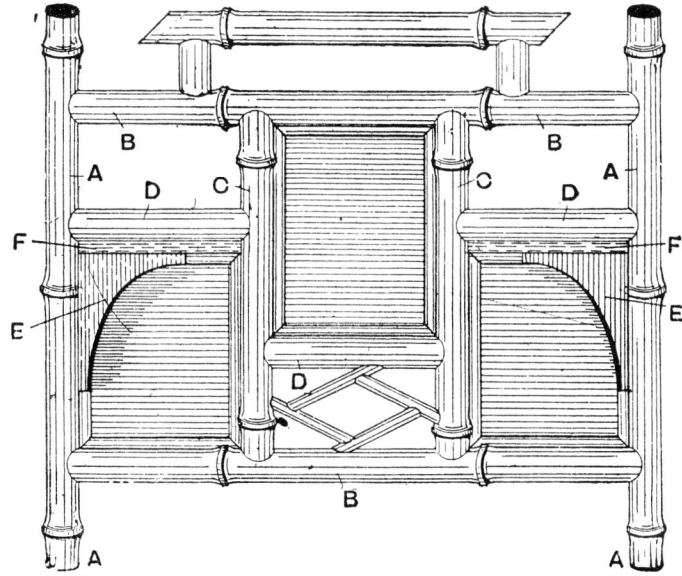

Fig. 157.—Bamboo Photograph-frame.

a cabinet photograph, as shown. From ½-in. wood cut out two pieces shaped as at E, and nail them on, slanting them forward at an angle of about 45 degrees. These pieces support the shelves F. For the beading, split some cane and nail it in, mitring the corners. Put a handle on the top, and screw on ear-plates to hang it by. For a picture frame, see p. 126.

A rack, arranged to accommodate ten pipes, the stem of each one being held in a piece of bamboo, is shown by Fig. 158. The frame measures 15 in. by 8 in. inside, the central rail being strengthened

by centre uprights. The ornamental work is optional; the bent work is made of thin bamboo or other cane. The pieces for the pipe holders should be about 4 in. long, with the knot close to the bottom end; and the supports for these should be dowelled into the frame.

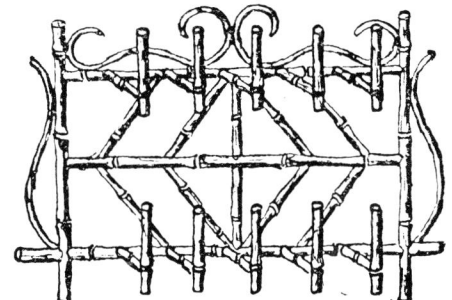

Fig. 158.—Bamboo Rack for Ten Pipes.

The rack shown by Fig. 159 is for nine pipes; the back frame is the same size as Fig. 158, but the centre rail or traverse is fixed lower down, as it forms part of the framework for the pipe rack, which

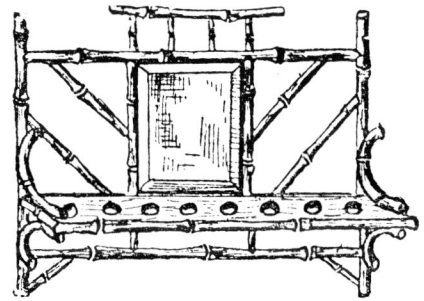

Fig. 159.—Bamboo Rack for Nine Pipes.

is a piece of thin wood about 2½ in. deep and covered with Japanese lacquer paper. Or the rack could be made of a piece of Japanese lacquer and enclosed in a framework of bamboo, the side pieces of which are dowelled into the back uprights, and further strengthened with bamboo brackets, top and bottom, either bent as shown or straight. In the back of

Fig. 159 a mirror is shown, but if desired this space could be filled in with lacquer or wood covered with Japanese paper. The framework of both Figs. 158 and 159 should be of ¾-in. cane, and the filling-in parts of ½-in. bamboo. In jointing, always use dowels where possible, but for filling-in pieces, plugged ends are strong enough; use glue for the joints, and further secure with a bamboo wire pin.

A four-fold screen frame, each fold being 6 ft. high by 3 ft. wide, is shown by Fig. 160. The screen could be made 6 ft. 6 in. high if desired, as the bamboos are imported that length; but a greater height

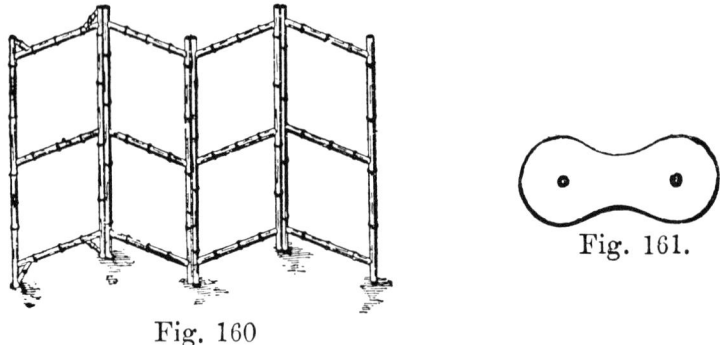

Fig. 160

Fig. 161.

Fig. 160.—Four-fold Bamboo Screen.   Fig. 161.—Screen Hinge.

involves a join, and screens are not usually required higher than 6 ft. 6 in. However, 6 ft. is considered the most suitable height. Eight 1¼-in. bamboos will be required for the uprights, with the ends plugged as far as is possible. It is assumed that it is the intention to cover the frame with some sort of material, so only three cross-rails or traverses are put in each, these being of 1-in. bamboo, dowelled into the uprights, the dowel being well glued in and secured with a bamboo pin on the outside. When the traverses are fitted to the uprights, say, of the first fold, clamp the fold up firmly with strong cord, getting it to a tight tension by twisting a wooden

stick in it (see pp. 23 and 24), and leave it until the glue is quite set; and so on with the remaining three. To give additional strength, short bamboo stays can be fixed above and below the top and bottom rails, as shown, the stays being plugged, cut, and rasped to shape, and secured with glue and pins. To hinge the folds together flat brass plates, as shown in Fig. 161, are fixed either with a brass-headed wire

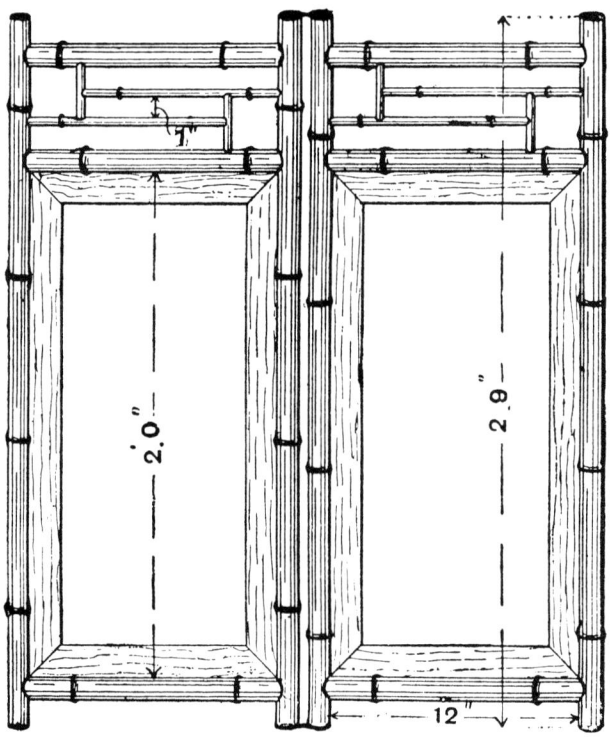

Fig. 162.—Two-fold Bamboo Screen.

nail or round-headed screw to both top and bottom of uprights, the end uprights being finished off with wooden buttons or terminals. Coat the work, when finished, with white spirit varnish.

A two-fold fire-screen is shown by Fig. 162. For this, three 1-in. canes and one ⅜-in. cane will be required. Cut off four pieces from the thickest end of the 1-in. canes, each 2 ft. 6 in. long, which will form the uprights, and six pieces, each 7 in. long, which allows 1 in. for the hollowing of their ends to fit the round surface of the uprights. One end of each rail must be fitted, first being hollowed as nearly as possible the same size as the cane itself. In consequence of the irregularity of bamboo cane it is necessary to fit each joint separately in the position it is to occupy. The rails and uprights should be marked with a saw-scratch, say, to prevent the possibility of mistake when gluing up. For the fitting of the second ends of the four cross-rails a

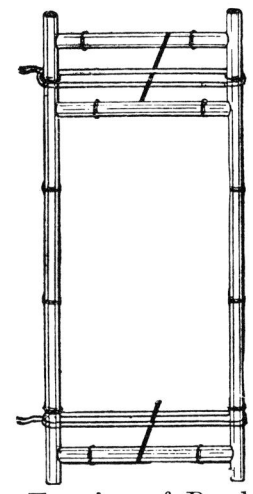

Fig. 163.—Framing of Bamboo Screen.

thin piece of wood must be cut 12 in. long to serve as a measure. One by one the rails should be placed in the position to which they are fitted, and the 12 in. marked off upon each with the assistance of the measure. In fitting the second ends, care must be taken that the hollows fall into the same plane as the first, otherwise they will not fit when the two uprights are parallel to one another.

Four bamboo canes, framed together into a square or oblong, form what bamboo workers call a " section." This is made clear on pp. 49 and 50. Much of the most important bamboo work consists in little

J

else than the framing up and filling in of sections and the fitting of them together. Accurate work is of the most importance in the framing up of sections; if they are not perfectly flat and rectangular, the error cannot fail to be noticed when the article is completed. Straight canes and true joints will secure the flatness of a section, and accurate measurements will secure its squareness. The two sections must now be framed up. The cross-rails are fastened to the uprights by means of wooden dowels or plugs about 3 in. long. The dowels should be fitted first to the cross-rails, then to the holes in the uprights. All the joints having been made to fit satisfactorily, the dowels must be glued first into the holes in the uprights. When attaching the cross-rails, it is

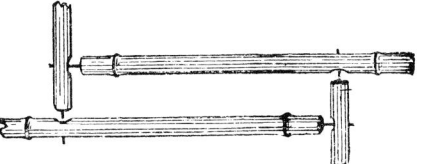

Fig. 164.—Filling for Bamboo Screen.

desirable to run a little glue into the tube as well as to glue the projecting end of the dowel, and for this purpose a piece of cane chamfered out at the end will make a useful gluing stick. The three cross-rails must be attached to one of the uprights first, the second upright being afterwards attached in the same way, and the whole gluing-up process done as quickly as possible. When the frame is together it must be clamped up at each end with string, as described on pp. 23 and 24, and illustrated by Fig. 163. After seeing that the sections are square, they should be put on one side for some hours to allow the glue to set.

The fancy filling work may be made from $\frac{3}{8}$-in. cane while the two sections are setting. Fig. 164 shows the construction; the four long rails should be cut off 12 in. long, and the short rails 5 in. long;

these should be hollowed out and dowelled. As these are for decorative work only, the pieces can be fastened together with fine panel pins. When the sections are thoroughly set, the fillings (Fig. 164) should be placed over the places they are to occupy, and the exact size for fitting marked off with a pencil. They should then be chisel-pointed, rasped, and fitted into their places with glue and fine beading pins.

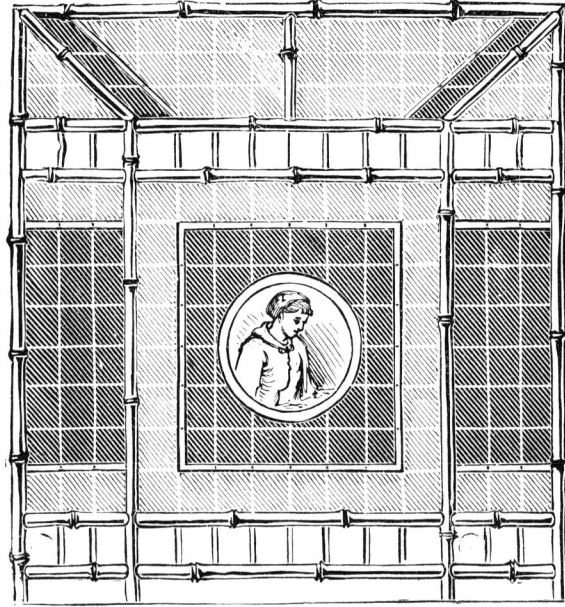

Fig. 165.—Elevation of Bamboo Fire-screen.

If the screen is to be filled with needlework, or any kind of work that requires stretching, a wood frame now should be made. The knots on the inside of the bamboo frame should, however, first be rasped down flat, so that the wood frame will fit in evenly. The wood frame can be fixed in by boring holes through the bamboo and fastening with fine wire nails. The small space existing between the wood frame and the bamboo should be filled with split rattan cane fastened on with beading pins, and

carefully mitred at the corners. If the screen is to be filled with glass, a rebate must be formed by fastening on split rattan cane. The glass must now be put into position and fastened in on the other side. The frame is now complete with the excep-

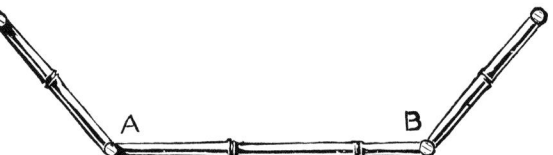

Fig. 166.—Plan of Bamboo Fire-screen.

tion of joining together and varnishing. The joining together can be done by two hinges made of tape, and fastened in a similar manner to the hinges fc a clothes-horse ; or by two pieces of brass, shaped as

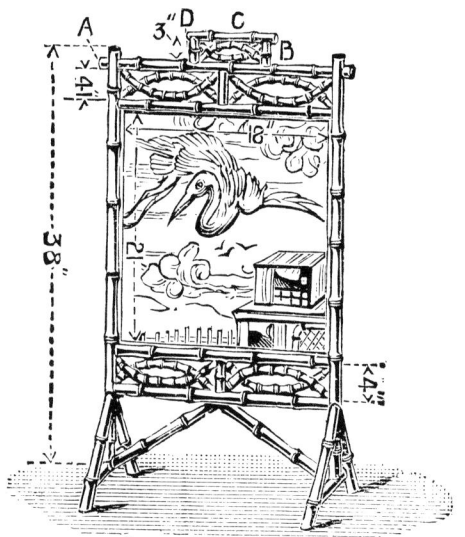

Fig 167.—Bamboo Fire-screen.

in Fig. 161, p. 143, fastened to the top and bottom of the inside uprights of each fold by screws, the hollow of the uprights being first plugged. The top now should be fitted with wood or metal terminals, and the whole should receive a coat of spirit varnish.

An elevation and plan of a fire-screen are presented by Figs. 165, p. 147, and 166, p. 148, respectively. The screen has a row of rails at top and bottom. A piece of iron bent to the proper angle should be screwed inside the framing at A and B (Fig. 166). The openings are filled with leaded glass, which can be fixed by narrow strips of bamboo screwed on each side. Mirrors or cathedral glass could be inserted in the openings if desired. If glass is not desirable, use silk or needlework stretched on light frames, or

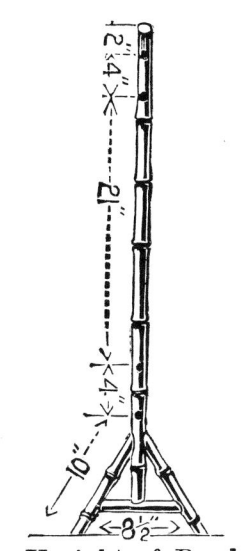

Fig. 168.—Side Upright of Bamboo Fire-screen.

the frames could be covered with canvas stretched tightly, and pictures pasted on; afterwards the pictures would require to be sized and varnished.

For the fire-screen shown by Fig. 167, use 1-in. bamboo canes. To make the legs, cut off two lengths, each 38 in., and two pieces 9½ in. long for the bottom stretchers, to make 8½ in. when rasped. Fit each stretcher to the bottom of the legs; drill holes in the centres of the stretchers, and fix dowels; then nail to the legs. Cut off two pieces 11 in. long, to make when rasped 10 in., and fit these for leg

supports; glue up, clamp, and leave till dry. With brace and bit, bore holes for dowels at distances, as shown in Fig. 168; the top hole in each side is to be bored through, and the dowel taken right through to hold the Oxford corner, as shown at A, Fig. 167. Cut four pieces, each 19 in. long, and rasp the ends to fit the legs; dowel, rasp two pieces, B B, 3 in. long, plug, and fit to the top cross-bar. Cut a piece, C, 7 in. long; plug this and fix to the top with glue and fine nails. Rasp two pieces to be 4 in. long, and

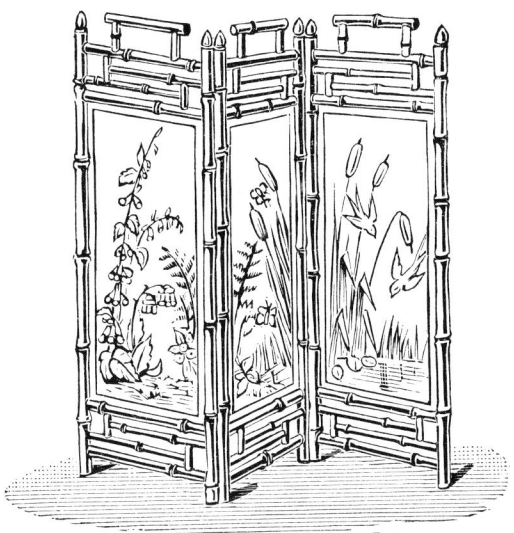

Fig. 169.—Three-fold Bamboo Screen.

fasten between the two top and the two bottom cross-bars. Glue and clamp the whole up with string or clamps. When dry—say in twenty-four hours—fix in the bottom supports and ornamental centre-pieces (which are made with thin Whangee cane) with fine French nails. Rasp off the knots where the panel goes and fasten in the panel with split cane. The filling-in of any screen may be with needlework, Japanese worked panel, lacquered panel, painted glass, or drawn silk, according to fancy.

A three-fold screen is shown by Fig. 169, and it

may have the following measurements : height 40 in., with inside 12 in. ; size of panels, 24 in. by 12 in. ; spaces between top and bottom rails, 4 in. ; use $\frac{3}{4}$-in. canes. Each section should be framed together as before described, and the small pieces between the rails must be made up before putting in. The fastening of the folds together is described on p. 148.

Another three-fold screen is illustrated by Fig. 170.

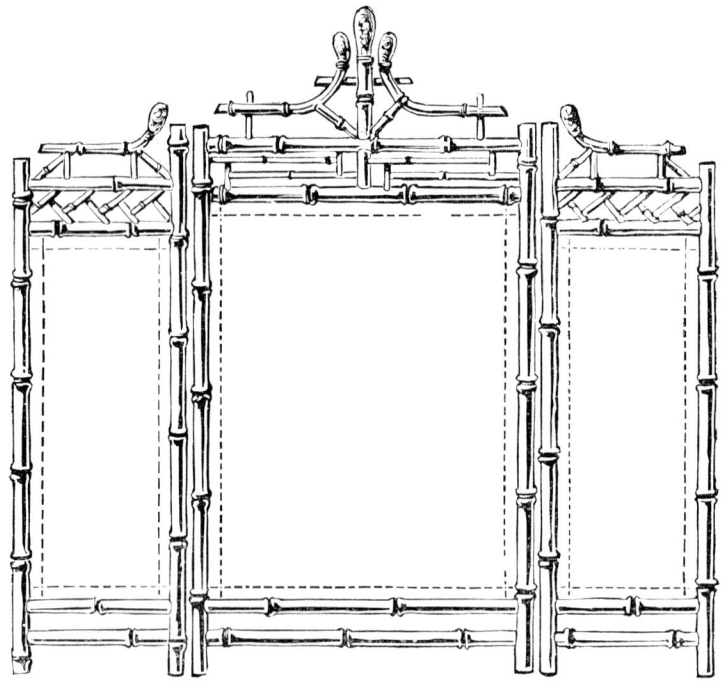

Fig. 170.—Three-fold Bamboo Screen.

1-in. canes should be used for the framework ; $\frac{1}{2}$-in. cane is suitable for the filling, and for all rooted work (except the centre root, which should be 1 in.). Suitable measurements for this screen are : four centre uprights, 40 in. long ; width for the centre, 28 in. ; outside uprights, 38 in. long ; inside width of outer folds 12 in.

A whatnot screen is shown by Fig. 171, p. 152 ; it has rooted bamboo, rasped down, for feet. The legs

should be made first. Fig. 172 gives lengths. Two Japanese lacquered panels, 18 in. by 10 in., can be used in this screen. The edges of the panels will be slipped with split bamboo, mitred at the corners, and fastened on with fine wire nails (two pieces of cane having first been nailed to the short sides in the form of a semicircle). This edging should stand very slightly above the surface of the panel. An angle will thus be formed to receive a beading of very thin cane, nailed in with $\frac{3}{4}$-in. panel pins ; this

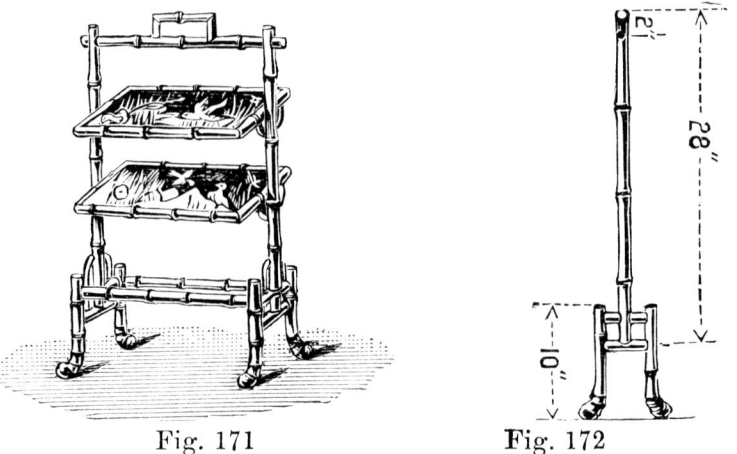

Fig. 171.—Bamboo Whatnot Screen. Fig. 172.—Side of Bamboo Whatnot Screen.

has been described before. 2-in. French nails should be driven into the centre of the 10 in. sides, projecting $\frac{1}{2}$ in., to form pivots on which the panels partly revolve. A very small hole should be made in each of the two legs, at distances of about 16 in. and 26 in. from the bottom, to receive the pins or pivots. Fit the top and bottom rails, dowel, glue, and clamp up. The tops of the uprights and any projecting ends of bamboo may be plugged, and turned wood terminals glued on to give a finish.

CHAPTER XI.

BAMBOO MAIL-CART.

ONE of the most popular applications of bamboo is in the construction of light, but strong, mail-carts. Bamboo is a material specially suited for this work on account of its elasticity and lightness.

Fig. 173, p. 154, is a side view of a single mail-cart, having a circular-shaped back; in front are two 8 in. wheels, enabling the mail-cart to be run on all four wheels. Fig. 174, p. 154, shows the wooden seat, and the position and number of the upright balusters and part of the shafts underneath. Fig. 175, p. 155, illustrates the rear end of the well, w, showing how it is let into the shafts, s s. This well is of wood, being finished at the edges with bamboo. Fig. 176 shows the manner of making the circular rail, R (Fig. 173), under the top bamboo rail T (Fig. 173), forming the body. This rail is $1\frac{1}{4}$ in. broad and $\frac{5}{8}$ in. thick, and its purpose is to secure the balusters in place, and to fix the bamboo rail over it. If the bamboo rail, T, can be bent properly, it may be fixed direct to the tops of the balusters without the intervening wooden rail, R (Fig. 173). The tendency, however, is for the upper rail to spread outwards, making an unshapely body. The springs are clearly shown in Fig. 173, the actual spring really being one piece from its end at E to the foot F; the other part, Q, is formed by the rods carrying the small wheels.

A pair of bamboo shafts, 4 ft. long and $1\frac{1}{8}$ in. thick, will be required; bend them to the form shown by Fig. 173. The handle portion of the bend, where the shaft dips slightly, cannot be shown in Fig. 173,

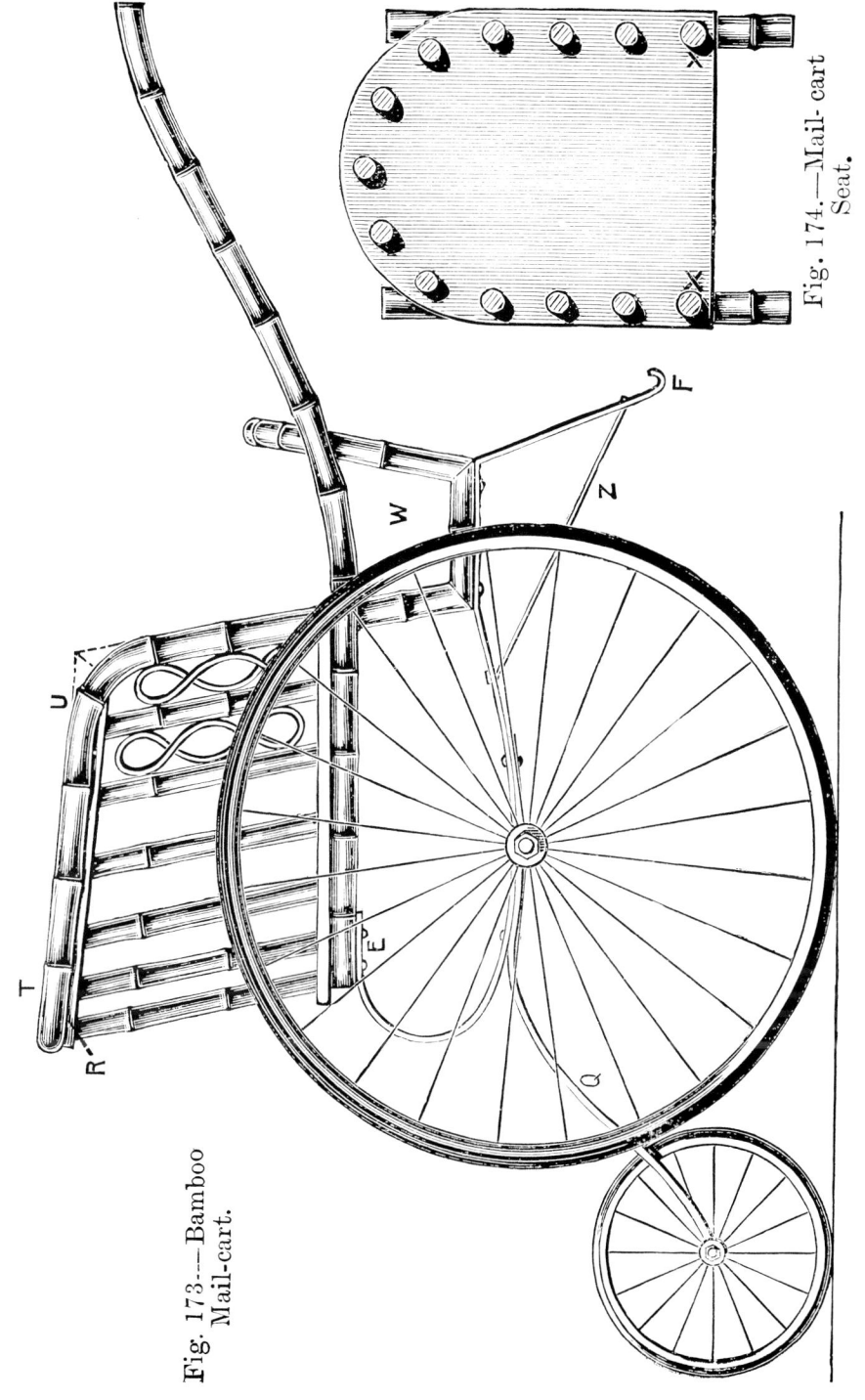

Fig. 174.—Mail-cart Seat.

Fig. 173.—Bamboo Mail-cart.

owing to limited space. When bent, the handles should be about 9 in. above the level of seat. Make a seat-board, 15 in. across, and the same from front to back, and $\frac{5}{8}$ in. thick, the grain to run across from shaft to shaft. The seat-board may be of pine, but preferably is of tougher wood, such as oak or ash. Cut the board to the shape shown by Fig. 174, and fix with screws on the under-side from front to back; a fillet of wood 2 in. wide by $\frac{1}{2}$ in. thick supports the circular end, which is unsupported by the shafts. Mark off the board for the baluster holes 1 in. from the edge. These holes are $\frac{3}{4}$ in. in diameter, and are bored only half through the board, with the exception of the two marked x x (Fig. 174), which go

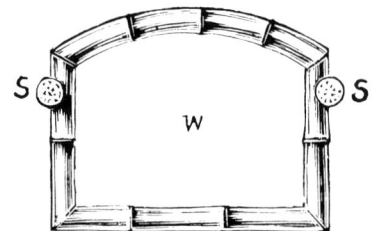

Fig. 175.—End of Mail-cart Well.

quite through, and fix the board to the bamboo shafts. Before fixing the seat-board to the shafts, the balusters forming the body are fixed in their places. These, as will be seen, are not of equal lengths; the height at the centre of back is $10\frac{1}{2}$ in., while at the rear end, u (Fig. 173), it is 9 in. The bamboo rail is in one piece all round the body, as shown at T, Fig. 173, its ends passing through the seat-board, and being wedged. If the bend presents great difficulty, the bamboo may be mitred, forming a corner; see the dotted lines at u (Fig. 173).

The well, w (Fig. 173), is made from $\frac{1}{2}$ in. wood, and is of a length to fit inside the shafts; it is 6 in. wide at top, and 5 in. deep. The inner face of the well is made to join the under-side of the seat,

where they are nailed together; the outer face (see Fig. 175) rises above the shafts some 3 in., and is curved, as shown. To the edges of the well the bamboo, $\frac{3}{4}$ in. diameter, is fitted by rebating, as is seen in Fig. 177, which represents a section of a rebated cane at a node. The bamboo is mitred at the meeting points, the top part being bent to the curve (Fig. 175); and is fixed on with fine wire nails. If a rail (Fig. 176) is made, it should be of a tough hard wood. It is of the same width as the seat,

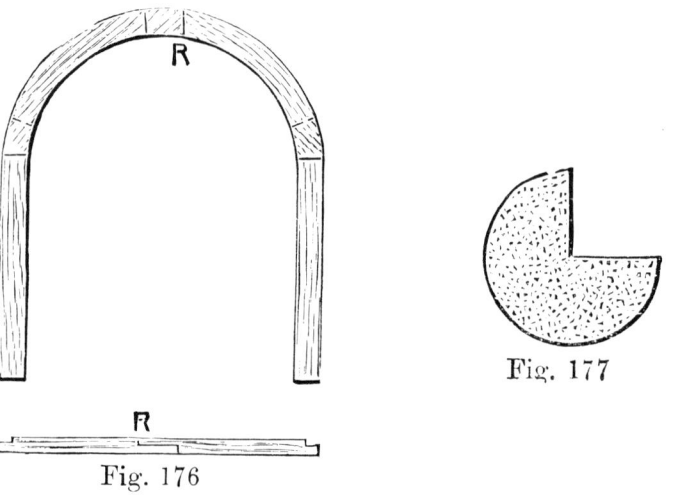

Fig. 176.—Upper Frame of Mail-cart. Fig. 177.—Section of Checked Bamboo.

15 in. outside measure, and divided the same as for the balusters, but it has two holes less at the rear end. Note that the holes, both in the seat and in this rail, must be bored with the brace on the slant, to allow the backward lean or rake to the balusters. In the length of the longest balusters this rake is 3 in. The rail (Fig. 176) is bored half through only, and when the balusters are cut and fitted into seat and rail, they are nailed with $1\frac{1}{2}$ in. wire brads passing through the wood into the ends of the balusters. For the top rail, T (Fig. 173), 1 in. bamboo

is bent to the shape of the wood rail, R, and fixed to it by fine $1\frac{1}{4}$ in. screws, passing through rail, R, from under-side. The ends of T, if made to descend to the shafts, are wedged in the seat-board. After the body has thus been completed, it is fixed to the shafts by screws passing through the seat-board, as above mentioned. The well is then fixed in its place, the bamboo being cut away to fit between the shafts, as shown in Fig. 175, S S.

The steel springs are 1 in. by $\frac{1}{4}$ in., set to the shape shown in Fig. 173, the axle being 6 in. from bottom of shafts. The springs at E (Fig. 173) are fixed by two screws to the ends of the shafts, and under the well, W, each by two screws. The leg, F (Fig. 173), is 9 in. long, and tied by a wire, Z, which is let through the leg, and through the spring a little in front of the well, W, where the end is turned over.

The larger wheels are 25 in. diameter, with $\frac{1}{2}$ in. rubber tyres, and the smaller wheels 8 in. diameter, also with rubber tyres ; the axle of the small wheels is fixed in eyes, and runs across the front. The wheels may be inside the carrying irons, or outside, at option. When placed inside, a small collar must be made on the fixed shaft, to keep the wheels up to the carrying irons. In Fig. 173 these wheels are shown on the ground line with the mail-cart level ; they should be elevated by setting up the irons till they are some 3 in. off the ground when the seat is level.

In Fig. 173 two compartments of the body are shown filled with $\frac{3}{8}$ in. laced bamboo or cane. These may be put in all the compartments or every second one ; they are bent, fitted in, and fixed with $\frac{3}{4}$ in. fine wire brads. The wood-work and cane may be varnished (the latter with white shellac spirit varnish) and the iron-work painted or enamelled, according to taste.